YOUR LIMITLESS POTENTIAL—AND POTENTIAL PROBLEMS—CAN BE UNLOCKED THROUGH THE ART OF NUMEROLOGY

In numerology there is no number as powerful as a Master Number. Beginning with 11 and ending with 99, these numbers—which should not be broken down—signify dynamic, "larger than life" aspects of your personality and affect every area of your life. They exist to guide you on a journey and help you know your higher self.

Korra Deaver shows how numerology works and how to find the numbers—including the master numbers—hidden in your name and birthdate. Going beyond the traditional Master Numbers of 11, 22, and 33 to reveal the Master Numbers 44 through 99, Korra Deaver shows how to use the secrets of numerology to make enlightened positive choices in every phase of your life—and avoid those situations that cannot ever work out positively for you.

TO KNOW THE HIDDEN SIDE OF YOUR SELF UNCOVER YOUR MASTER NUMBER

THE MASTER NUMBERS

A New Approach to Understanding Yourself through Numerology

by Korra Deaver, Ph.D.

Library of Congress Cataloging-in-Publication Data
Deaver, Korra.
The master numbers : a new approach to understanding yourself through numerology / Korra Deaver.
p. cm.
Includes bibliographical references.
ISBN 0-89793-128-9: $7.95
1. Numerology. 2. Symbolism of numbers. I. Title.
BF1623.P9D38 1993
133.3′5—dc20
93–12012

Cover Design: Beth Hansen   Book design: *Qalagraphia*
Project Editor: Lisa E. Lee   Editor: Jackie Melvin
Production Manager: Paul J. Frindt
Marketing: Corrine M. Sahli   Promotion: Robin Donovan
Customer Service: Liana S. Day
Publisher: Kiran S. Rana

Manufactured in the United States of America

9   8   7   6   5   4   3   2   1   First edition

This book is dedicated to Jereme, whose name numbers provoked, or, rather, pushed me into researching the mysterious, unexplored Master Numbers.

ACKNOWLEDGMENTS

For many years Master Numbers 11, 22, and 33 were all that could be found in numerology books. Almost nothing had been written about the numbers from 44 to 99 except for Faith Javane and Dusty Bunker's *Numerology and the Divine Triangle* (Whitford Press, 1980). They gave delineations of the numbers to 44 and, at the back of the book, worked with all the Master Numbers in relation to tarot and astrological correspondences, along with personal vibration references. Dusty Bunker also made a beginning with the higher Master Numbers in *Numerology and Your Future* (Whitford Press, 1980).

After I was well into the writing of this book, I discovered that Faith Javane had written a most interesting update, *Master Numbers, Cycles of Divine Order* (Whitford Press, 1988), in which she explores the esoteric values of the Master Numbers. She has done some outstanding research from Blavatsky, Baily, and other esoteric writers.

But no author yet, that I have found, has considered the influence of the higher Master Numbers on the four numerology chart divisions individually: Birth Path, Vowel Total, Consonant Total, and Full Name. *The Master Numbers: A New Approach to Understanding Yourself Through Numerology* is a correlation of work already done in the simple numbers with ideas as to how two basic numbers may work together to create the Master Number. I cannot claim originality for the traits assigned by tradition to the numbers developed in this book—a six is a six with all of its designated characteristics, no matter in what combination it is found. The references at the end of a paragraph indicate the authors and their works, listed in the bibliography, whose ideas helped to develop that thought. I hope that this very basic beginning will inspire other numerologists to enlarge upon this work with their own thoughts and research.

CONTENTS

1

===

The Basics of Numerology

While this book focuses on the Master Numbers, I want to begin with some fundamentals of numerology in general. Those who already know how to draw up a basic numerology chart may want to skip this section. No new material about the basic numbers will be found here, except, perhaps, for a comparison of the Pythagorean and Chaldean systems or the explanation of how a baby is named.

The science of numerology is as old as recorded history. It delves into the influences of the vibrations of numbers. It is a method for understanding some of the tools we have brought with us to achieve the psychological and spiritual goals we have set for ourselves in this incarnation.

Names play a vital part in directing and influencing our destinies. Bible teachings repeatedly bring out the importance of the vibrations of names. In Genesis we were given the power to name everything within our environment. The Lord often changed the names of chosen people to more closely represent the task or service they were to carry out.

The Aquarian Age has already begun, and it will reflect a higher rate of vibration than the age we have just passed through. Ahead of us are difficult and turbulent times as the vibrational rate of the earth changes to meet the new age. If we are to make it through the transitional period ahead with a minimum of difficulty and maladjustment, we must get into harmony with our own vibrations, working with them rather than against them, and travel at the rate that belongs to each one of us individually.

The vibrations that most closely affect you are determined by your recorded name at birth and the day, month, and year you were born. Each letter has its own number; each number has its own meaning. The science of numerology tells you how to adjust to the things that cannot be changed, or, by making the changes within your power, attract to yourself the situations, people, and events that will best help you.

Numerology translates the letters of your name and birth date into the numbers 1 through 9. Each number represents a quality of character. We each work with all nine numbers. How we use them creates harmony or inharmony in our lives. The missing numbers from your birth name (numbers that do not appear) also play an important part in computing your total strengths and weaknesses.

There are four main influences in your numerology chart: the Birth Path, Vowel Total, Consonant Total, and Full Name.

The Birth Path is found from the sum of the numbers of your birth date. For example, if your birthday is January 23, 1943, your Birth Path is 5. January (1) + 23 + 1 + 9 + 4 + 3 = 41. Then, 4 + 1 = 5.

The Birth Path has been called by various authors the Life Path, Soul Path, Life Cycle Number, Destiny Number, Life Lesson Number, and Birth Force. It is your essential Being, what you are or have at birth even before you are named, the special gifts you have that will help you accomplish your destiny. It shows what lessons you must learn in this lifetime, what past-life lessons you have learned, and what qualities you can rely on to help make your way in the world. It states what you have to your credit—your character, traits, and talents—and is most useful in shaping your choice of a career.

The Birth Path cannot be changed and shows the direction you must take whether you want to or not. It shapes your life and your environment. It is very strongly tied to the way you direct your life and your experiences and will likely overshadow or channel the energies of all other numbers in your chart.

66 is the highest Birth Path to be obtained in this century. The highest combination of birth numbers available comes from

December 31, 1999, and this total is only 71. It remains for the numerologists of future centuries to discover possible Birth Paths with higher Master Numbers.

The Vowel Total is called by various authors the Soul Urge, Motivation Number, Mental Self, Inner Self, Heart's Desire, or Soul Number. It creates desires and urges for activities in both the inner and outer worlds, a yearning for self-expression at the highest level within you. It has much to do with your feelings, thoughts, and actions, your attitudes towards things and people, your judgments, your principles, your point of view—it is generally your motivating force. It is what you want to do and be, what you express to the world. It can create a very strong personality, sometimes becoming so predominate as to seem to obscure the influence of other numbers. It is found by the sum of the vowels in your name.

The Consonant Total is called by various authors Quiescent Self, Impression, Personality Profile, or Heart Self. It has been described by numerologists as both the quiet, passive self, concerned only with your own dreams and aspirations, and as the impression you make on others. I consider it the psychic self—not the outer personality that is readily seen and understood but the inner self that is felt by your family and closest friends, that part read and understood by the psychic self of others. It is the growth aspect of the Soul, the avenue through which it participates in everyday activities—watching, learning, being aware of daily challenges; thinking, making and storing decisions from each experience. It is identified by the sum of the consonants in your name.

Your *Full Name* has been called the Expression, Destiny Number, Outer Self, Prophecy Number, or Path of Destiny. It is your purpose for this incarnation, your spiritual mission, your reason for existing, what you must do or be in this lifetime to succeed. It is your field of opportunity, defining what you must give of yourself to others and to Life, and suggesting what kind of people you should meet and work with. Here you will find the natural capacities given to you by the vibrations of your name, your talents and possibilities, and the type of work in which you might be most comfortable. It shows what you can do. It is not what you are. If you change your name, you will move in harmony with the vibrations of the new name, and your possibilities will change also. The full name is found by the sum of all the numbers of your name. (3)

Sometimes these influences are at odds with one another. What you want to do may not fit what you are doing, and constant interferences create frustrations, doubts, and fears. Sometimes a change of name will help, but don't change your name at random. Follow your instincts, or study numerology. If a name feels good to you and you vibrate with an inner joy when the name is spoken, it probably is a name that will attract much good to you. A study of numerology will prove it out. (3)

When doing a basic numerology chart always use the full birth name *as spelled* on the birth certificate. Name changes in marriage, work, or signatures are a separate form and should be compared against the original name. Additions such as Sr., Jr., II, III, Mr., Mrs., Ph.D., M.D., or other degree letters are not considered by numerologists as having numerical value even if found on the birth certificate. Also ignored by numerologists are titles such as doctor, professor, Esq., president, etc., even when always used in a signature. St. or Saint before a name (such as St. John or Saint Augustine) is a title and is considered an addition. If, however, a person's last name is St. John, (such as Anita St. John), then the St. or Saint is counted as part of the numerical values. If Saint is shortened to St. on the birth certificate, then use that form.

Your birth name is a record of experiences brought from past lifetimes and will influence you all of your life. These are the vibratory influences you were born with (or without). They indicate the overall plan for the expression of this lifetime. They reflect your essential nature. Other names may accentuate other qualities, but the strongest underlying influence will always be the birth name.

Can a birth name be given to you in error? Yes, this occasionally happens, but usually the incoming Soul has a name for itself that is gradually impressed upon the parents during the nine months before birth. Psychologists are coming to understand that memories, even prenatal memories, can be invoked under hypnosis or during regressions to past-life or inbetween-life experiences. For example, when an attempt was being made to dislodge entities attached to a woman, one entity identified itself as her next child, and called herself Krystle. The woman was delighted and would not allow this entity to be banished. About a year later, she gave birth to a child whom she called Krystle. When this ability to probe into the inner mind is understood more universally, it will become a common practice to ask the incoming Soul what name it prefers to be called by, and fewer mistakes will be made.

Even if an error is made, the vibrations of the birth name create opportunities for situations that influence us all of our lives. To mitigate this, most of us have a second name. It may be a nickname, a business name or initials, or a woman's married name. This change, whether great or small, comes about through Soul growth or changing aspects of one's individuality. As one fulfills the inner needs expressed by the Soul at birth, changes take place in the personality. Often these are reflected in nicknames or even deliberate name changes. Women often choose a married name that gives added strength or stability to their original path or fulfills a missing number. On the other hand, some marriages dissolve because the vibrations of the new name are incompatible with the Soul's needs, and the frustrations and inharmonious conditions which result are unbearable. If you create a numerical chart past middle age, you will quite likely be surprised by how your life has been shaped by the vibrations of your name at birth, how life's experiences have strengthened the missing qualities, and how the potentials have been fulfilled.

There are two ways to determine the number values of your name: the Pythagorean, or "Western" method, and the Chaldean method. The Pythagorean method is the one most used today. It assigns number values thus:

1	2	3	4	5	6	7	8	9	11	22
A	B	C	D	E	F	G	H	I		
J		L	M	N	O	P	Q	R	K	
S	T	U		W	X	Y	Z			V

The number values are added together. For example,

$$
\begin{array}{cccc}
6 & +5 & & = 11 \\
R & O \quad G & E \quad R & \\
9 & +7 & +9 & = 25\ (7) \\
& & & 36\ (9)
\end{array}
$$

Totals are broken down and added together, except when a total is a double—or, Master—number (11, 22, 33, etc.) So, 11 + 25 = 36. The 11 stays as is. 2 + 5 = 7. 3 + 6 = 9. In the name *Roger*, we read: Vowel Total 11, Consonant Total 7, and Full Name Total 9. This example is for simplicity. You will usually be working with two or more names (first, middle, last) when doing numerology charts.

The Chaldean method was part of the early "mystery" school teachings and assigns the number value by sound, which uses the concept of vibration and gives a numerical designation to each vibrational pattern. It does not use the number 9, which was considered to contain all vibrations. Thus, our current alphabet would have these values:

1	2	3	4	5	6	7	8
A	B	C	D	E	U	O	F
I	K	G	M	H	V	Z	P
J	R	L	T	N	W		
Q	S		X				
Y							

The basic psychological or spiritual value of each number remains about the same in both systems, but, as you can see, the totals will be different. You might try figuring your name both ways to see which fits the plan of your life more accurately.

And here is a very brief synopsis of the basic psychological aspect of each number:

1 – The individualist, pioneer, loner

2 – The companion, teammate, committee person, facilitator

3 – The artist, sculptor, aesthetic, self-expression

4 – The worker, duty-bound, steadfast

5 – The traveler, globe-trotter, loves experience

6 – The server of family or community

7 – The hermit, contemplative, introspective

8 – The manager of money, time, resources, talents

9 – The humanitarian, sage, counselor

If this is your first contact with numerology, I would advise you to study any or all of the books currently on the market for more information about the basic nine numbers.

Your own Soul Self awaits you!

2

A Backward Glance

I hated my birth name—Cora Leatha Hughes. I was named after my father's sister, Leatha, and half-sister, Cora, both of whom he adored. Despite the affection involved, aesthetically speaking, he couldn't have found three names that fit together less well. All three began and ended in an expelling of breath. Just to speak my name left me out of breath. (I could say it left me breathless, but that doesn't have the same connotation.)

With Vowel Total 4, and Consonant Total 4, my life was unremitting hard work, restricted and bounded in discipline and responsibilities. In school I was alone—studious, awkward, gangly. I must have been a colorless child because I had neither friends nor enemies, so I immersed myself in study and found companionship in teachers and other older people who had something of value to say. And how I loved to listen and learn! Born August 11, 1923, my Birth Path number was a 7. I made good use of those searching, contemplative qualities, graduating fifth from the top of my class at 16, after only ten years of schooling.

My life in the grownup world was little better, although once out of school, I began to make friends and have a social life of a sort. But I always felt that I was a day late and a dollar short when it came to self-fulfillment. Nothing ever really jelled.

Finally, after three unsuccessful marriages, which gave me three wonderful daughters, that Secret Self which had patiently bided its time until family responsibilities had been nearly fulfilled began to push—hard! I realized that if I didn't change my lifestyle, I would remain stuck in a circular rut, forever going nowhere.

When my youngest daughter, Lydia, started high school, I started college. As a wife, mother, student, and full-time breadwinner (not necessarily in that order of importance), it took four years to get my first 2 year college degree, an AA in English/Journalism. Lydia and I graduated the same year from high school and college. We even got our pictures in the papers, wearing our mortar boards with tassels on the left, as mother/daughter graduates.

I was a three-time grandmother, aged 45, and no one needed me anymore. Wonderful freedom! My husband and I had very little in common; the only thing we found of mutual interest was our children's activities. So (as I am fond of saying whenever appropriate, and sometimes when it isn't), when my children reached 18, *I* left home! Taking my car, my clothes, and what books I felt I couldn't live without, I went down the road one day and forgot to come back. I left with my husband our mobile home and what few possessions 21 years of marriage had given us.

I didn't know what life had in store for me, or even where I was going, but that inner push by the Secret Self could no longer be denied. I had to find out what was missing from my life! There were only two things I knew for certain. In my late thirties I'd become interested in metaphysics, and I was sure that my destiny was somehow tied up with that fascinating field of study. The second thing I was sure of beyond the shadow of a doubt was that I was going to change my name!

My home was on the West Coast, and since I couldn't go any farther west without driving into the Pacific Ocean, I headed east. I had with me a list of metaphysical centers, all five that existed in 1969. Somewhere I knew there was a place for me. As I traveled, I experimented with signing my name in different ways, searching for that certain something. I tried various spellings, even adding a "Van" to the name Deaver, which my husband said had been dropped some generations back when his family arrived in America from their Dutch homeland. Nothing clicked.

Then one day as I neared the Atlantic seaboard, the name

Korra fell with a flash of light into my mind. I cannot describe the powerful feeling of release that surged through me. I felt as though an ages-long burden had been lifted from my shoulders. The whole world looked happier, more prosperous, more full of light and love. It was a spiritual revelation, bringing a kind of exultation I'd never experienced before. I remembered that Saul of Tarsus, too, had seen that flash of light (albeit much stronger) on the road to Damascus when his name had been changed to Paul.

At the next stop, as I signed my name Korra Deaver, I knew this was the name that was right for me. Some years later Paul Solomon, a trance psychic in Virginia Beach, told me Korah had been my name as an English Druid, and that it meant "Daughter of the Sun." Well, that certainly was appropriate! I am a Leo with five Leo planets in my horoscope and I could never be more a daughter of the sun than I am in this lifetime.

All of this happened before I had even heard of numerology. I continued my search for my own special place in life, but none of the metaphysical centers I visited felt right for me. Some weeks later I found myself ready to stop for the winter, half-way back across the continent in Little Rock, Arkansas. I had been wandering around the United States for eight weeks, not needing to be anywhere in particular, just relaxing and trying to find peace within myself.

Following my inner guidance, I found a wonderful old southern mansion and, before the winter was out, I was inviting teachers and students into my home for classes in yoga, astrology, meditation, and all the things I wanted to learn about. Such teachers were few and unskilled in those days, but I felt if the teacher was one lesson ahead of her students, she could at least teach what she knew and the student could take it from there.

Three years later, in 1972, two partners and I incorporated The Institute of Psychic Science, later renamed The Parapsychology Education Center, a school which developed and certified teachers in all the psychic sciences. There were not many books on psychic or metaphysical subjects then, but to provide the students with at least what was obtainable, we also established a bookstore. Among the inventory I found four books on numerology: *Your Days Are Numbered* by Florence Campbell, *Modern Numerology* by Morris Goodman, *Numerology, Its Facts and Secrets* by A. Y. Taylor and H. W. Hyer, and *Numerology* by Vincent Lopez. That was all that was available to me on the subject in those days. Working out my own name, I discovered my destiny, and I understood why I had struggled so long to be free of the name that bound me to the sterner side of life.

Numerology did not become an instant consuming passion for me. I was much too interested in finding, developing, and following the inner guidance for my own life, which I gradually learned to recognize as Soul Consciousness, that state of illumination that makes obscure things plain to understand. (This is explained in my book, *Psychic Power and Soul Consciousness*, Alameda: Hunter House, 1990.)

Once a year the center held a fund-raising psychic fair. As president, resident manager, overseer of teachers, bookstore operator, and twice-a-week teacher of metaphysics, I did not have the time or inclination to develop skills as an astrologer or other reader, and, besides, the center was developing plenty of those. So, for my part in the fair, I chose the little-known practice of numerology. It was easy to memorize the meaning of the numbers, to figure name and birth date, and to give the customers a quick numerology reading. Everyone seemed to be satisfied.

Except every once in awhile someone with a quicker thinking capacity—a little less frivolity, a little more skepticism, perhaps, or a little more eager to get at the truth—would challenge my "reading," pointing out that what I had just said did not fit their life at all! Integrity and honesty are two qualities which I treasure most, and these "misfits" always threw me into a tailspin. I certainly did not want to be considered a charlatan, even though I was a novice, as were most of us in those days.

Then I noticed that most questions contained their own answers. When I told one woman with a missing 7 in her birth name that she probably had trouble in school, she icily informed me that she held several college degrees and had spent most of her life in various fields of learning. Suddenly, with that illumination I learned later to cherish, I understood that the missing numbers of a birthname represent blank spaces to be filled in by the owner's life experiences and that she had been performing her spiritual duty. Though I tried to explain my new revelation, she was in no mood to be mollified and left my table in a huff, presumably to find a more talented "reader."

I also realized that the missing 4 in my birth name held more significance than I had given it credit for, and that although the vowels actually added up to a Master Number 22, the definition of 22 did not fit the life experiences I had known, while the lesser value of 4 certainly did.

Never one to stop with only partial information, I continued to study missing numbers and Master Numbers in the numerology charts I did. It became increasingly clear that a missing number usually will override a Master Number with the same breakdown value, when life insists you learn the required lesson. A missing number is a spur, a kick in the pants, the necessary impetus to keep us moving along the path of spiritual evolution. I found that if the possessor of the Master Number has *any* missing number representing lifelong lessons, the impact of the Master Number will be considerably lessened. This is especially true if the missing number is the Master Number's own base. Only when I had earned the right to say I understood the meaning of merciless dedication to duty and could recognize order and plan in my life as requested by my missing 4 was I freed to experience other values.

Although my new name had completely different values (Vowel Total 9, Consonant Total 1, and Full Name 1), the birth number 22 became a predominant factor in my life. The drudgery of the 4 gave way to the joyous Master Builder, as Helyn Hitchcock said about the 22, "learning to be both practical and inspirational." (4)

Although missing numbers are not really within the scope of this book, I feel that if parents focused more attention upon the missing number values of their child's name they could help speed up the growth factor represented there and allow the child to reap the full benefits of the Master Numbers more effectively. By the same token, I wouldn't recommend deliberately giving a child a name with no missing numbers. The person who has no missing numbers has nothing to struggle against, so that the life represents a time of rest, of lesser action, and consequently lesser growth. The name that delights the parent at birth is most likely the one that is in harmony with the incoming Soul. In my case, only the spelling was at fault. "Cora" and "Korra" are pronounced the same, and my father could not distinguish the difference in meaning.

Master Numbers have been regarded with awe by numerologists, and thought to be given only to special Souls who are ready to use their spiritual qualities for upward leaps of consciousness. That may be true, but the sad fact is that, for the most part, the possessors of Master Numbers must still live in and cope with this world as it is. Because of their sensitive nature they seem especially aware of and kicked around by the degradations of the rest of humanity, and some of their own.

It also has been thought that the higher the number the higher the consciousness, and that few people on Earth today are spiritual enough to rate a consciousness higher than 33, often called a Christ Consciousness.

Neither of these assumptions are necessarily true. One doesn't think of the numbers 1 to 9 as growing more spiritual because an 8, for instance, is higher than a 3. Each number simply represents a *different type* of human consciousness, each uses different abilities and has different characteristics. As we incarnate from lifetime to lifetime, we must encompass the qualities of all the numbers, and Soul growth comes from the expansion of awareness and wisdom which arises from the diverse experiences created by the attributes we are currently working with.

The same is true of the Master Numbers. A 66 is not more spiritual than a 22 or a 44. They are different from one another in the same way their basic counterparts are different. A Master Number is "higher" only in the sense that it reflects an expanded or more aware state of consciousness than its own base. A 66 has a broader and more sensitive awareness than its lower version of 3, but it still takes on the artistic characteristics of the 3, while adding a double dose of the community awareness of 6. Similarly, a 44 basically reflects a larger version of the management-conscious 8, while adding to that an extra awareness and the control that belongs to the restrictive and duty-conscious 4.

Sometimes this expansion of consciousness creates extra notes of conflict to be resolved by the individual. How does the introverted, contemplative 77, for instance, cope with its extroverted, ever-changing base of 5? Or the globe-trotting 55 deal with its scientific, pioneering 1? There's enough material here to keep numerologists (and psychologists) happy and busy for a long time.

In my experience, it has been more rare to find a chart without a Master Number than with one. Perhaps because of my position in the Parapsychology Education Center, and as a teacher of metaphysics, the people who sought me out were people who were already seeking a higher consciousness of life, so my experience may not be typical.

More than one Master Number in a name, however, is much more rare. Two or more Master Numbers produce the person who is not only highly spiritual, philosophic, and philanthropic, but extremely sensitive spiritually and emotionally. The potential is there for great involvement in the affairs of humanity, but, in fact, the extreme sensitivity generated by these Master Numbers quite frequently sends the person into retreat, unable to cope with the harshness and the pressures of the outside world. Then the individual is more likely to live out his life under the influence of the basic numbers, allowing the true magnificence of the Soul to shine through only occasionally. Alcoholics, drug addicts, suicides, and others on the dark edge of human experience often have two or more Master Numbers in their charts, testimony to the extreme pressures and tensions the individual must endure.

The parents of such a sensitive child have a special and unusual job, that of guiding their spiritual prodigy through the maze of childhood traumas without destroying the uniqueness of the Soul. They must strengthen the child's belief in Self without enhancing ego, teach understanding and forgiveness of others without destroying self-worth, and awaken altruism for all humanity without fostering self-abasement. Truly a prodigious undertaking!

The child should be encouraged to spend time alone, not as a punishment, but to read, meditate, write letters, or simply stare at the wall, whatever is needed to give the mind rest and to create peace and tranquillity—to find that inner place where the gateway into Soul Consciousness is opened. All bearers of

Master Numbers should make time to be alone frequently.

(I've never had the opportunity to do numerology readings for persons confined in jail for long periods. Might not this be an escape from the pressures of a difficult life? The Soul, too sensitive to endure the rigors of the world, would find a kind of security where it is fed, clothed and sheltered, and where decisions are made for it. In this case, jail would be a type of hermitage where one is allowed long periods of solitude for contemplation and rest. Approached from the eternal point of view, a study on criminal numerology could be quite illuminating.)

It was the name numbers of 5-year-old Jereme that finally pushed me into exploring the higher Master Numbers and, as so often happens when required to do something, Soul Consciousness came through with the key to deciphering them. Named Jereme Thomas Van Drielan at birth, his numbers add up to an awesome Vowel Total 11, Consonant Total 77, and Full Name 88! What a challenge it's going to be to raise this spiritual prodigy! Will he be able to live up to the potential inherent in his birth name, or will he fall by the wayside as I have seen so many bearers of Master Numbers do? As one man crudely put it, he can be either an astronaut or an asshole. Well, one doesn't necessarily exclude the other!

In one way, I'm glad the shaping of this spirited young life is in the hands of his capable and energetic young parents, but in another way I'd like to live long enough to have a hand in the stew once in awhile, and see how this child of the future turns out.

3

Master Numbers—Their
Similarities and Conflicts

11, 22, 33, 44, etc., as I have said, are not broken down. These Master Numbers indicate a larger, more spiritual concept of Life than their lesser totals. Each number has both positive and negative influences, because nothing is all positive or all negative. The qualities of the Master Numbers are intensified and they are far more powerful than the nine simple numbers in both negative and positive aspects.

I'd like to discuss the manner in which these higher Master Numbers are found. I picked up several bad habits in the early days of idly dabbling with numerology charts for curiosity seekers. One notion is that the 9, or numbers that add up to 9, such as 5 plus 4, cancels itself out and can be ignored when one is adding for totals. One will never find a total higher than 33 by using this method. Another shortcut that provided erroneous information for me was adding the individual names separately, and then further breaking down the resulting two-figure total. This, too, will bring only low totals. The two-figure totals of each name should be added together.

The only successful way to provide correct information on a numerology chart is to add all the numbers from all of the names together. By this I mean add all of the vowel numbers together, and all of the consonant numbers together, using 11 rather than 2 for K and 22 rather than 4 for V. From these resulting totals, which will likely be in the higher digit figures, you can instantly see when a Master Number turns up.

Let's use this fictional name to show all the steps: breaking down the totals to the final single digits, or by adding only whole numbers:

```
   2           + 4           + 2          = 8
   11          + 22          + 11      = 44 = 8
  6 + 5   + 1  + 6 + 9 +6     + 5 + 6   = 44 = 8
R O G E R   A N T O N I O   M c D E V O N
9 + 7 + 9   + 5 +2 + 5   + 4 +3+4 + 22 + 5  = 75 = 12 = 3
   25          + 12          + 38      = 75 = 12 = 3
   7           + 3           + 11      = 21 = 3
```

You can see by this example that the totals could be read as:

Vowel Total	8
Consonant Total	3
Full Name	11

or they could be read as:

Vowel Total	44	
Consonant Total	12	= 3
Full Name	56	= 11

In one reading we get two Master Numbers, and in the other we only get one Master Number.

One usually adds the reduced Vowel Total and the reduced Consonant Total to find the Full Name number. This is correct, but one should also add together the unreduced totals from the vowels and consonants. For instance: Vowel Total 21 becomes a 3 and Consonant Total 23 becomes a 5. Together they add up to an 8. *But* add the 21 and 23 together and you have the Master Number 44! Do *both* sets of addition when working out a chart to be sure to find all Master Numbers the person is entitled to.

This is also true of Birth Path totals. Add the number of the month, day, and year in this way: December 15, 1950 as 12 + 15 + 15 equals 42. No Master Number here, so the Birth Path is 6. But November 18, 1988 added together as 11 + 18 + 26 equals 55! And December 30, 1959 added as 12 + 30 + 24 equals 66! Wow!

On our Soul's journey through eternity each of us reaches mastery in small increments, over many incarnations. Expanded consciousness comes about through added emphasis on certain types of experience. In each lifetime we perfect one small thing, such as kindness, virtue, love, integrity, the use of material laws or the use of spiritual laws, or the combining of both, until the aggregate creates an example dazzling enough to open the eyes of others to the beauty we have achieved. Many Masters are incognito even to themselves. The perfected quality no longer has duality—that is, to love or not to love is no longer a question; the Master of Love is love personified—so there is no reflecting counter-quality by which the Master measures him or herself. Most are too intent upon pursuing their own inner development to recognize the effect their presence has on others. In their pursuit of expanding consciousness, their only aim is to help others. They would never knowingly harm another being, but sometimes the only way to clean out a sore is to cauterize it. Our lives must be cleansed before they can be healed, and sometimes the cleansing process of confronting a Master is painful and confusing.

How do you know when a Master touches your life? Like a guru, they can make the incomprehensible comprehensible. They open up vistas of understanding never remotely considered before. They have the capacity to clear away stumbling blocks in your own consciousness. Many times awareness of that clearing away takes place after the Master has come and gone, as one's consciousness finally grasps the full implications of what was done or said. It is important for us to remember that no one is our enemy and no one is our friend—all persons are our teachers. It is a sad loss to stand unaware in the presence of a Master and let the opportunity go unrecognized.

The true mission of the holder of Master Numbers is that of service to fellow beings, each in its own way and in its own field. They represent a journey into oneself, a seeking for spiritual power and control over the lesser nature, and all have highly sensitive and introspective characteristics. But just because you achieve Master status doesn't mean you become so spiritual you lose contact with your humanity. In fact, one is apt to be even more conscious of one's faults and thus fall into the opposite trap of self-flagellation. Maintaining high ideals against the inertia, or even active opposition, of the rest of the world is the real challenge to the holder of Master Numbers.

Should Master Numbers be considered a blessing or a burden? Master Numbers, as with most other things in life, are what you make of them. They are vibrations of tremendous power and energy, which push us to the limits of our emotional and spiritual resources. They require considerable control and direction, for the negative qualities of the Master Numbers can be far more destructive than the negative aspects of the other numbers and can bring much unhappiness to the holder if allowed to do so. A Master climbs out of the pit of his lesser nature into the sunlight of positive, constructive use of the energies at his disposal. When constructive use is consistent, without relapses, the Mastery in that area is complete and the Soul goes on to the next area that must be conquered and transmuted into virtue.

Holders of Master Numbers expect more of themselves and set their goals higher than the average person, which may explain why they fall so far when they do not live up to their own expectations. They are subject to more extremes in emotions and actions. They are aware of more conscious choices. They can have great high-mindedness or an equally powerful loss of ethics.

Few of us achieve the greatness our potentials promise for us. Most, like the desert rose, are destined to bloom unseen, or have a small sphere of influence; but when used at their highest energy level, the positive qualities of the Master Number can have far-reaching potential for good, and can even lead to honors and fame. Within each number lie great Soul choices. In our journey through eternity, we will travel both the high road and the low road in order to correctly recognize and assess the perfect balance. Experiencing both the positive and the negative characteristics of all the numbers and all the combinations of numbers is necessary for spiritual growth and understanding as we make our way through many incarnations towards full Mastery.

4

=

11—VISIONARY
OR DAYDREAMER?

"Jereme, if you have two lines like this"—I drew an 11 on his paper—"what would you do with them?"

"I'd draw a well, add two crossbars like this, and make a ladder to climb out of the well with."

Interesting. That's what an 11 does. It climbs out of the well of the 2 personality into the headier air of enlightenment.

Jereme has a Birth Path 11 and Vowel Total 11. Maybe, with that clear thinking so typical of young children, he instinctively realizes that this is what his Soul has decreed for him in this lifetime. Does he see himself as climbing out of a well of dark experience, or does he see himself as having access to the deep well of wisdom bought by that experience? Only time will tell.

While the world could not progress without the willingness of the 2s to put a shoulder to the wheel, the Soul Consciousness of every individual knows we cannot remain stagnate forever. We must "arise and go unto our Father"—stop accepting crumbs and sit at the table to feast from the viands of an expanded view of life. In a real sense, every Master Number is the Soul rising like a phoenix out of the limitations of its own base number.

An 11 is sensitive, dreamy, and high-minded. 11 is often called the number of revelation. The holder of this Master Number loves to delve into the hidden mysteries and causes of situations and events, even of life itself. These personalities are inclined to be withdrawn socially and are seldom understood or fully appreciated by their associates, reaching as they do to a more universal consciousness. It is not easy for them to drop their viewpoint to common levels just for the sake of socializing, so they live more within themselves than in the external world.

On the positive side, they demand and display high standards in thought, work, and play that few people can live up to. The Soul's test of the holder of Master Number 11 is for the development of honesty and integrity. A lie will always be revealed. Insincerity will always be exposed. This is a sort of cosmic testing to determine their spiritual worth.

The premise for Master Number 11 is: 1 + 1 = 2. 1 is the individualist, pioneer, loner. 2 is the companion, teammate, committee person, facilitator. Key words for an 11 are: Self-Illumination Through Spiritual Inspiration.

BIRTH PATH 11

If you hold an 11 here, your Birth Path is one of revelation, enlightenment, and maybe even the possibility of reaching Soul Consciousness. Introverted and idealistic, you are the mystic, the dreamer, the visionary. You act upon inspiration, and during this lifetime you learn to rely upon intuition to sharpen your insight and to inspire your resourceful and inventive mind. You often receive clairaudient and clairvoyant guidance, though you may have to learn to become aware of it. You are intensely interested in philosophy, mysticism, occultism, and ceremonial magic, and it is your job to discover what type of illumination or revelation it will be your privilege to share with others. (1, 3)

Humanitarianism arises from your very soul, and you could become nationally or internationally known if you devote your energies to the service of humanity, for the 11 vibration is intense, exciting, and electrifying. But if you attempt to act for self-glory, your own energy will be turned back on you. Remember, there is a difference between notoriety and fame. To be valuable and real, fame must come to you when you are not searching for it. Walk boldly and with assurance, but let recognition come to you naturally. Do not seek it. Don't become egotistical about your power, but realize that whoever would lead must also serve. Others will be inspired by your example if you live the Truth that is revealed to you, living humbly in spite of public attention. (1)

Time is apt to have little or no meaning for you, as you are inclined to live in your own world and to travel to the beat of your own drummer. You are more at ease in the outdoors or wherever you can be free from the restrictions of schedules or appointments.

Life's Lessons for Birth Path 11

You are driven by your Soul Self to develop honesty and integrity. Lies and dishonest practices will always come back to you and you cannot work for selfish purposes without disastrous results. Truth must be the primary objective if you are to develop to the highest spiritual power you are capable of obtaining. This power is awakened through gracious, loving, and selfless service to others, given freely wherever needed. Look for the best in others and for the good that can come out of all situations and circumstances. (9)

This life is basically meant to be a search for spiritual understanding, but you can do with it as you will, and your returns will come accordingly. Inspiration and a desire for Truth will help you develop the right use of the psychic world, learning how to handle its powers and how to share your discoveries for the benefit of others. In our ongoing evolution, the subconscious, conscious, and Soul minds must be trained to work together, and this is the spiritual goal you are striving to attain. (9)

The mental, inner-directed life is the source from which you draw your strength and wisdom, but do not lose sight of the fact that you must live a material life as well. A distinctly practical side must be developed in order to make your idealism function in the world. You are not required, however, to accumulate or hoard material things. Everything comes when needed. The number 11 protects its own, and you will never be in want. If you gather possessions, fame, or money for their own sake, your potential for humanitarian action could be submerged in materialism and lost to you and the world. As a result you could become miserly, egotistic, sly, and condescending. (3)

Your most rewarding opportunities will arise out of the living and the teaching of Truth as you see it and in sharing the knowledge you find. This could be along spiritual or occult lines of thought, in the world of invention or acting, in the study of spiritual philosophies, in contact with and in paying attention to the inner guidance from your Soul Self. (1, 9)

VOWEL TOTAL 11

To tell the world about the beauty you have discovered in the depths of your own spiritual experience is your heart's desire. You believe that the world would be a happier place if all persons understood *your* concept of God and how necessary it is to live true to the ideals that uplift humanity. Searching for spiritual enlightenment has probably been your direction for more than one lifetime, and in spite of many unanswered questions, you are intrigued by the mysteries of mortality. Idealistic and intuitive, you have great ideas with universal possibilities, and the experiences created by your unfolding spiritual consciousness lead to wisdom, which you try to share with others. The dreamer and the visionary, you'd like to save the world, but what you must remember when trying to inspire and transform humanity with your vision of Truth and Beauty, is that all spiritual growth comes from within. It cannot be imposed from without. (1, 5, 9)

Your feelings towards others are kindly, and persons from all walks of life come to you as a source of strength and inspiration. In your estimation, the current state of affairs leaves much to be desired, and you work always to create a better future. You are devoted to salvation and spiritual growth, but you love your ideals more than you do your fellow beings. Right is right, you always say, regardless of individualities. It will be helpful if you remember that some people may not understand your type of thinking. (1, 9, 11)

You can develop far-seeing vision through the cultivation of prophetic and other psychic powers. You may be clairvoyant and clairaudient, receiving visions from sources within yourself. People find you sympathetic and insightful, with strong spiritual aspirations. You are ambitious and vital, and your mental capacity is unlimited. Follow your hunches and feelings, for your Soul's guidance is sure. No goal is beyond your reach. (5, 11)

You have great inner strength and the courage to face and to cope with the changes and surprises through which life challenges you. Your mind is active and alive to new ideas and is capable of unusual creativity, which needs to be put to useful ends. You often use more than one avenue of release for your inflowing ideas and are always striving for balance in the working out of all of your current projects. Your thoughts, both positive and negative, emanate strongly from you and are often felt and responded to by those with whom you associate. (1, 11)

Helping Yourself with Vowel Total 11

Choose your friends, mates, and partners from among persons with other Master Numbers, because no one else is capable of living up to the ideals you set for yourself and for all of humankind. Winning friends and influencing people comes so naturally to you that you are valuable to any organization or partner. From these sources you can draw more down-to-earth people whose talent can help you implement your elevated visions. (9, 11)

Your greatest need is to develop denial of self and tolerance of human idiosyncrasies. Even though you would rather be with people of your own kind, that does not help you to understand those on the more general level of humanity. To fulfill your most desired goals, you must better know those whom you wish to help. Your life force flows from the spiritual and the refined and you proceed along an idealistic intellectual line, but unless you have closer contact with those who have less intuition than you, you may not know how to help them. (5)

Since time has so little meaning for you, it is inevitable that you are frequently late for appointments, but once present you give energetic vitality to whatever you are involved in. Your inner world may be out of sync with the real world, but remind yourself that you still live in this one and must adapt yourself to its ways.

Keep your emotions on an even keel and stay cool when others don't accept the revelations you receive or see the same kind of beauty in the world as you. Believe in yourself. All the wonderful things you dream of will some day come to pass, but it's part of your mission to help make them happen. The bonuses of life are seldom handed to us on a silver platter; they are the just rewards for work well done. (9)

CONSONANT TOTAL 11

Endowed with qualities of leadership and inspiration above the ordinary, and ahead of the majority in the mental, emotional, and spiritual aspects of life, you have a divine mission to preach the "gospel" to the world. Through your eloquent oratory you lead many to the Truth, as you see it. You strive always to become more enlightened so that you can be a guide leading people towards faith, understanding, and greater spiritual awakening. About you is a luminous energy that inspires people to work toward unfolding their own possibilities, drawing strength and courage from your example. (1, 9)

You get along well with people of all kinds. You believe in and work for equal opportunity, no matter sex, race, religion, or station in life. Within your heart is a grand dream to be a great inventor, to be the one who leads the way into a new era. Let your energies flow through altruistic aims and purposes, for all efforts come more easily when goodwill, love, virtue, and selfless service are your guiding lights. (9)

You are interested in the occult and the metaphysical and may become a well-known psychic, perhaps a seer who can foretell national and world events. Divinely inspired visions, dreams, omens, and coincidences fuel the flames of your need to interpret the meaning of Life. (9)

Because your intuitive nature allows you to sense "wrongness" or faulty interpretation of religious creeds and dogmas, you may become an agnostic in your early years. However, your generally optimistic nature works best when you explore metaphysical/spiritual principles from the positive side and use them for the highest good of all concerned, not only in yourself, but also in your relationships with others. (8)

The seat of compassion within you is deep and must be exercised in order to develop your own happiness. You will be wise beyond your years when you recognize that your inspirations and strong insights are invaluable in solving life's difficulties. In all activities, seek for revelations that will help you to understand the purpose and meaning of your life, and do not allow your intellect to smother or block the development of intuition and vision. (8)

You have an air of elegance which touches the inner nature of those around you. Your inventiveness creates your own specialized style in artistic endeavors through which you may achieve recognition and fame. You dress with flair and originality, and you may create your own fashions. Being different is your style. If you keep your aims high and your mind and emotions positive and constructive, there will be more advantages than disadvantages in your life. (11)

The Negative Side of Consonant Total 11

Take care that you don't become so much of a dreamer that the practical side of your life becomes submerged. If little details command too much of your attention, you may lose contact with reality. You may become egocentric, scattering or ignoring the many gifts with which you are endowed. Beware of karmic retribution if you become unjust, prejudiced, or intolerant. Using power harmfully always whiplashes back upon the holder of a Master Number.

If you don't live up to the best that is in you, people will find you shallow and artificial and may consider you a hypocrite. You may have a tendency to dramatize or to exaggerate things in word, manner, or deed. This can create wrong impressions, even if you exaggerate in the positive. To avoid this, keep a level head and be realistic in your approach to people, problems, and goals. Seek nothing for yourself, but devote your life to the service of humanity, and people will seek you out, drawn by the purity and brightness of your soul. (1, 11)

FULL NAME 11

When at your best, you convey a spiritual quality that inspires others to find their way out of the darkness. A sunny and optimistic attitude toward life is your natural demeanor, so that you brighten the world around you. Your powerful intuition penetrates into the deepest secret. You are the idealist supreme, who envisions a superior and evolved future for humankind. You are an insightful thinker and enlightened philosopher, an advanced artist, a producer of ideas that others less tuned into universal truths can catch hold of and translate into practical reality. But, in spite of your high and wonderful visions, you must learn to keep your feet on the ground or your dreams will never bear fruit. Your attention span can cover more than one thing at a time, but you may need the help of more practical people to charge your ideas with reality. (5, 9)

Because you have so many outstanding talents and because good things flow so easily through your life, you are inclined to expect the same from others. Remember not to expect others to enjoy the elevated views that are the natural forte of the person with a Full Name 11. Others must shine from whatever level they find themselves, and it's up to you to teach them about your philosophical point of view. Take a moment to go back and start from where the other person is now, if you wish to win and hold their support and admiration. (10)

With an inborn talent to see all sides of the question, you have the ability to create harmony and balance between opposing interests. Quickly taking in the situation, you can see what should be done next and mediate to everyone's benefit. Because you enjoy contrasts and harmony and all the nuances inbetween, you can be tempted to go to extremes just for the experience, experimenting with both the physical and mental senses. Black magic, alcohol and drug abuse, and all of the darker side of life are also within your reach, for you could turn your attention to the left-hand path as well as the highroad to spiritual growth. An antidote for either smug superiority or callous indifference is to remember that all you send into the lives of others comes back into your own. (5)

You are known by the company you keep. Highly sensitive and psychic, you can be swayed by influences from lesser personalities. Mix with people who have worthwhile goals and ideals to keep your own aspirations high. Learn to listen to your own intuition. It's easier to correct a mistake from your own judgment than to undo the misdirection of another.

Failure to grasp and fulfill the opportunities available through this spiritual number may cause you to live your life as a 2, which will be more restricting. You may then discover you are being used as a doormat, walked upon and pushed around by other people's whims. An 11 must learn that the only path to spiritual growth lies in service to others. But do it because it is the right thing to do, not just because you don't know how to say "No." (4)

Opportunities for Full Name 11

A natural promoter, advertiser, and teacher, you feel right at home in the limelight. Radio, movies, newspapers, television, magazines, acting, and writing can be made to work for you. Although it is possible to achieve fame or recognition in some way, do not let it become an end unto itself. You are a visionary, and since you have an inclination towards communications and philosophies concerned with the uplifting of heart and soul, you might find use for your talents in the fields of religion, the occult, or psychic experimentation. You are happiest when you can inspire others with your elevated outlook, and you might find a loving way to serve through a gift of prophecy or other extrasensory powers. (5, 10)

Your best chance for recognition is in the arts or creative professions. You could find your niche in community affairs and work to make better living standards for those less fortunate. You function best in activities that call for insight, discernment, and decision-making ability, but where time is not a decisive element. Although you have a lively personality and capacity for leadership, you're too impractical, high-strung, and dreamy for the stresses and objectivity of the business world. If you seek employment there, look for jobs that are free of deadlines and time schedules. (9, 10)

POSSIBLE VOCATIONS FOR ELEVEN:

Advertiser, artist, astrologer, astronaut, astronomer, attorney, auctioneer, author, beautician, biographer, booking agent, campaigner, character analyst, composer, computer expert, congressperson, critic, dancer, educator, electrician, electronics expert, entertainer, filmmaker, graphologist, healer, judge, leader of inspirational movement, magician, masseur or masseuse, mayor, mediator, medium, metaphysician, missionary, musical director, musician, organizer or promoter of cooperative movement, painter, photographer, playwright, poet, postal worker, priest, psychic, psychiatrist, psychotherapist, publicist, publisher, radio announcer, revenue collector, salesperson, scholar, sculptor, social worker, telephone operator, television repair, youth worker. (12)

5

===

22—POWERFUL
OR POWER MAD?

"Jereme," I mused aloud, "today we will work with the 2s."

Jereme looked up from the rug where he lay sprawled with his fleet of cars around him. "Aren't they the people who get into things?" he asked.

"No," I chuckled, "you're thinking of the 'Terrible Twos.' I'm talking about the 22s who are a little more rigid in action than the Terrible Twos, but who can stir up just as much activity to set the world on its ear."

22s are apt to be eccentric. They have large purposes to fulfill and tend to go about this in unorthodox ways. The Soul's demand is for the development of positive and constructive use of energy, and they gravitate toward the larger machinery of governments and movements where they can serve the greater number of people. To work for selfish purposes is to court disaster. The challenge for 22s is to develop patience, discipline, and determination that bring about spiritual rulership over material forces. Consequently, they are more interested in principles than in people individually. (1)

22s are involved in a broad range of activities, including every field that works toward the progression and uplifting of humankind. Many advancements and new techniques in art, science, and philosophy have been created by holders of this Master Number. (7)

Power-full or power-hungry? Their inner drive is to learn

to manipulate substance. Right or wrong, they stand for the dream realized, bringing vision and ideals down to the material level. No one has yet defined how far genius is from madness.

The premise for Master Number 22 is: 2 + 2 = 4. 2 is the companion, teammate, committee person, facilitator. 4 is the worker, duty-bound, steadfast. Key Words for 22 are: Self-Mastery Through Self-Enterprise.

BIRTH PATH 22

A Master of the material, you have the power to get things moving, and you delight in showing how to put the cosmic laws of the material and physical world to beneficial use, to invent new ways of applying old principles. New ideas spring from your ability to make improvements on and to further develop the work of others. With your unlimited creativity, you can help bring any project to a grand conclusion simply by focusing your tremendous energies toward the desired goal. You have a strong leaning toward mysticism. You use your insights to bring psychic and spiritual principles down to a practical level and, conversely, you can make the useful and practical into something splendid and uplifting. (1)

The work you do provides a foundation upon which others can build better lives or a stronger society. You drive yourself hard; achieving the goals you set for yourself comes before all else. To bring your dreams to fruition, learn to view life from a broad perspective and to function well within large organizations, possibly on a national or international scale. Politics, business and industry, and movements that promote philanthropy and world peace are areas ideally suited to your talents. (7, 8)

If these very powerful energies are abused, you could become ruthless and dictatorial. You could be further restricted from realizing your higher potential by grandiose dreams of self-glorification which would lower your magnificent 22 to the more mundane level of the 4. (3)

Life's Lessons for Birth Path 22

In this lifetime, you will learn to develop reason and diplomacy, to correlate the physical with the inspirational, and to put these qualities to tangible use for the benefit of humankind. Balancing the spiritual with the physical requires focusing your mind on the details of the project while still preserving your highest ideals. As an added incentive to achieve these things, you may have been born with a physical or mental disability for which you must learn to compensate. (4)

Idealism, practicality, and depth of understanding permeate your actions. You have a good grasp of the mechanical side of things, whether it is organizing information for a book, restoring an old car, or promoting a huge fundraising affair. You know just which steps to take all along the way. Although you use esoteric wisdom to create your goals, the world sees the tangible result. Your greatest achievements in life come when you set out to help humanity in a positive and constructive way, and so you must develop philanthropy, tolerance, receptivity, and bold initiative.

Being a leader comes naturally, and you could have unparalleled power, as your abilities cover a wide range of activities that could become international in scope. Within you is a desire to build, to create in a larger-than-life fashion. You may be an innovator, developing your own business that provides service on a large scale. (4)

You command respect and could put your inspirations to work in such areas as international movements, large commercial, educational, or political institutions, affairs of government, churches, charities, etc. Your lesson is to learn to use your organizational ability to work with large-scale projects to bring about greater good. (1)

The desire to use this power to aid others will show you how to accomplish what you envision. "Find a need and fill it" is a motto for prosperity, so if you remain always cognizant of what is needed by those around you, your inspirations will provide many ideas that can be helpful to others and prosperous for you. Your works can affect the whole world if you think and act with all of humanity in mind, and you may even achieve historical fame for a major humanitarian work you have founded, invented, or established. (9)

You would delight in traveling to distant places and meeting with persons of high rank or authority. Consider your talents and abilities when looking for the best fields in which to use them and do not let your ideas fall short of what you are capable of doing. Let your dreams rise to truly grand concepts and for best results, choose a field that requires ultra-specialization. (9)

VOWEL TOTAL 22

You have more challenging goals than most people, for your life's work is to make the world a recognizably better place. The urge from your soul is to be the true Master Builder, building for permanence rather than for prestige. You build structures, both tangible and intangible, that have a lasting impact upon the lives of others. Even if you are esoteric rather than pragmatic by nature, the philosophical bridges you build create permanent change in the lives of those you touch. The most advanced and enlightened concepts of art, philosophy, science, and economics keep your mind fine-tuned and always constructively busy. (1, 5)

You have balance, autonomy, vision, leadership, love of people, desire for progress, and the managerial ability to make your ideas work. The things you build, whether esoteric or exoteric, must, above all, have service and practicality. You feel that there should be a reason for anything, and that even inspirational, spiritual concepts must have practical application. Though you behold high visions, your feet are firmly planted on the ground. You are the practical idealist, using reason and diplomacy to work your way to the top. (1)

You have a high desire for perfection and you are not comfortable unless the things you do are as good as you can make them. You are patient and gentle, but have the power to command. You love people and give willing service whenever called upon, restoring peace and order in your unique and special way. Spiritual and progressive, you are self-confident in any activity that you engage in. (9)

You use imagination and natural leadership to create improvements in all the areas you touch, and you work for enlightenment wherever the seed can be sown. You would make an excellent counselor because you never betray a confidence and you have the objectivity to see all parts of the whole, which gives you the ability to arrive at workable solutions. People respect you because they recognize your fairness and trustworthiness. Your inner guidance can be trusted to give you right judgment and good counsel, so protect your beautiful ideals by keeping them safe in your heart where they cannot be swayed by others. (1, 9)

Helping Yourself with Vowel Total 22

Position and prestige can come easily to you and if you follow your Soul's urge, you will use the wealth you can gain from successful enterprises to fight ignorance, corruption, and brutality. You belong to the public and your resources are people. You have the vision to see how money and people can be organized on a far-reaching, even worldwide scale and create for yourself a place of power and influence. Keep in mind, however, that this kind of power could be hazardous to your spiritual safety, and unless you would see your work come crashing down around your feet, remember that great responsibility goes with great power. (5, 8,)

Regardless of your Master status, you are still a human being and are subject to the limitations and fallibilities of human nature. Don't lose sight of your objective to maintain a high degree of steadfastness and idealism in the midst of materiality, conflict, or frustrating situations. You always give others the freedom to follow their own dreams and ideals, but don't forget you have a great destiny also. You have the power to accomplish monumental and lasting works, so do not sell yourself short. Faith can do things never done before if it is strong enough. Follow your star into great and important activities. (3, 9)

CONSONANT TOTAL 22

This vibration is strongly charged with both physical and mental energy, and it should make you a very energetic person. If life has not stifled it, you should also have a lot of ambition. This will be very helpful, for ambition can act as an energizing force to all the good influences in your character. (11)

22s are active in many different arenas, always devising new concepts and new inventions that benefit great numbers of people. You have wonderful dreams of how peoples and races can be united into constructive or uplifting activity. The huge construction areas of the world attract your attention and you break through the barriers of stultified tradition to find new and better ways to create great energy and transportation systems; you design factories and industries with new, sturdier, and more beautiful buildings that incorporate efficiency, cleanliness, and improved working conditions; you improve agricultural, communication, and exchange systems; and you invent ways to produce better products. (1, 9)

You have the potential to become an internationally known figure who gives time and money to charities and special interest groups that parallel your own lines of thinking. As a skillful negotiator who can meet any situation with tact and diplomacy, you could make such sweeping and penetrating changes as to reshape the course of nations and industry. Using reason and logic, you spend your efforts to bring about better understanding among nations, working to make your ideals of world peace and unity come true, directing great affairs of state, becoming an ally of the people of all countries. (9)

To make this powerful Master Number effective, the petty worries of daily living should be sent to the back of your awareness. Put your energies where your dreams are. You have the capacity to provide service in a huge arena. Nothing you do is simple. You must dream greater dreams and achieve greater results than the average person. (7)

You have an intuitive understanding of the needs of others and the charm of an inspiring, loving, and magnetic personality that brings hope and cheer to those around you.

If you keep your emotions positive and optimistic, extend

an unqualified love towards all people, and cultivate kindness and mercy, life will reflect the same back to you. You are a hard worker, ethical and honest in your relationships. Whatever you do, you do well, and you can become an expert in any field you select. The practical aspect of all things, even spiritual things, is always emphasized. The persona of being "too heavenly for any earthly good" will never be found among the 22s. (7)

The Negative Side of Consonant Total 22

If you have a negative side, it may show up as ineffective action because you cannot balance your ideals (the sensitivity of the 2) with reality (the practicality of the 4). (3, 8)

Self-knowledge is important to achieving your very best. Knowing what makes you act and react is necessary if you want to accentuate the positive while overcoming the negative.

If restrictions multiply too rapidly, you may become cynical and feel that the majority of people are unthinking, self-centered, and uninspired, and you may come to the conclusion that no one is capable of understanding your dreams and large concepts. To get financing, you might turn your attention to get-rich-quick schemes, usually to your downfall. Beware of letting frustrations tempt you into boastfulness or giving grudging service. At such times it's more important than ever to maintain your high ideals and to keep your dreams and goals polished bright.

Unlimited power used indiscriminately could cause you to become power-hungry and seek to use people for your own benefit, becoming self-serving and indifferent to the feelings and rights of others. Forgiveness, understanding, and impersonal love will help you keep your priorities straight. Give your energy without reservation to the selfless plans you envision and the results will be magnificent.

FULL NAME 22

This Master Number has a strong promise of success, of complete effectiveness in the use of power. You can make or break yourself or others, so you must be constantly aware of the need to exercise caution and ethical discernment. You are continuously charged with nervous energy and radiate power from both conscious and unconscious levels. This energy can best be kept in control by directing it into activities that benefit others. You know how to put great ideas into action, especially those that arouse and help humankind. You are the one who pioneers new fields and opens them up for the good of all by providing the groundwork upon which others can build, especially in areas where cooperation between people is needed. (8, 9)

There are always some hardships in every life, for in working through difficulties the Soul develops strength, intuition, and wisdom. However, you have the happy ability to take all this in your stride and seldom think of adversity as an obstacle, preferring, instead, to think of it as a preparatory step along the way. Others look to you for guidance because they recognize the keen insight you have into human nature. You make an excellent mediator, especially as you get older. Having grown to understand yourself from your own wide experiences, you understand how to blend the opposing views of others. (10, 11)

You will become inhibited and suppressed if you live your life in too narrow a scope. Keep your viewpoint broad and your interests wide by traveling to different parts of the world. Travel will also provide an active outlet for your inexhaustible energy. In your ambition, you can overwork and bring on physical and emotional disabilities, so don't overdo it. You need to give freely, but you also need to conserve your own strength and substance in order to continue to serve. Take time to be alone and replenish your energies. (10)

Opportunities for Full Name 22

Organization is your greatest talent. You plan your work and work your plan, and you make it a challenge to get things done speedily and well. You have a special aptitude for coordination, bringing together ideas, people, or things into a more productive and better organized whole. Working alone does not succeed as well for you as contact with groups. Large works and exciting new projects that catch the public attention easily draw your participation. You can establish national or international activities and efficiently follow all aspects of the project, beautifying while you build. Bridges, hospitals, museums, and great learning institutions are the types of monuments you leave to the world, whether you participate in the actual construction or work behind the scenes to mastermind fundraising, paperwork, or create public interest. (1)

You understand the process of turning ideas into tangible form. Blueprints, dress patterns, story plots, or any set of instructions hold no mysteries for you. You can see the end from the beginning, the entire picture with all the details of the process. Whether the project is large or small, you know how to calculate the needs in energy, finances, and numbers of people. Any goal you can conceive you can achieve when you put your tremendous energy into it.

The power you wield carries with it great responsibility and, if you do not live up to your best self, also houses great destructive powers. Administrative and policy-making capabilities are second nature to you, but a ruthless craving for wealth and power can lead you into criminal activity, possibly ruining yourself and damaging others. You must guard against malpractice because you will touch many, many lives. Those holding Master Numbers receive a direct backlash from lack of responsibility. Your rewards will come in direct relation to how successfully you serve your fellow beings.

If, instead of undertaking larger duties for the benefit of the community or the world, you hide your light in small, self-serving tasks, your magnificent 22 will reduce to the drudgery of a 4, and you will find yourself hemmed in and restricted by detail and routine. If you find yourself bound by duty, limitations, and the need to rebuild your resources, use your perseverance to push yourself up and out into a larger field. Lift your eyes to the brightest star and life will carry you far toward fame and fortune! You have the knowledge, the understanding, and the power to carry out your dreams. (10)

POSSIBLE VOCATIONS FOR 22

Accountant, advertiser, aeronautics and positions in space, agriculturist, analyst, anthropologist, appraiser, architect, athlete, aviator, bank inspector, biologist, booking agent, business executive, cartographer, chemist, claims adjuster, collector, corporate lawyer, critic, dancer; director or organizer of cooperative movements or businesses such as chain enterprises, labor unions, political causes, professional sports, public works or utilities, racing meets, or world tours; draftsman, dramatist, economist, engineer, explorer, factory supervisor, fiction or sports writer, foreign goods buyer, geophysicist, healer, importer/exporter, insurance agent, international financier, job counselor, journalist, landscaper, large-scale manufacturer, law or trade expert, lecturer, legal secretary, master mechanic, mathematician, military officer, musician, nurse, orchestra leader, personnel advisor or director, physician, politician, printer, promoter, psychiatrist, psychologist, real estate agent, researcher, school official or educator, secret service agent or chief, stage manager, supervisor, surgeon, theatrical producer, translator. (12)

6

===

33—MYSTIC OR MARTYR?

My friend Charley, whose Birth Path is 33, said, "33s love to help the people around them," and he's right. He spends money and time doing thoughtful little things for anyone whose needs come to his attention. Service to the larger arena of humanity appeals to 33s as well, ministering to spiritual needs and the elevation of human consciousness. Not surprisingly, Charley works as a healing channel for the Martinists, an international esoteric movement.

Long thought to be the highest consciousness humans could attain, 33 has been elevated by numerologists nearly to divine status. With this expansion of human consciousness comes a revelation of a broader compassion, love, mercy, and justice that can be called upon to aid others in the unfolding of their spiritual paths. The greatest challenge for 33s is to focus their emotional attention on spiritual goals. This will help to develop much-needed balance and stability in their own emotions and judgment.

The Soul's demand of the holder of a Master Number 33 is for the development of kindness and altruism. Those who need heart's-ease and encouragement easily sense the empathetic nature of the 33. By responding willingly and lovingly to the needs of others, 33s find direction for their own spiritual growth. To accomplish this successfully, they must learn to live with a detached but caring attitude, which makes it possible to touch and heal the deep misery found within many human hearts without transferring destructive pain to their own psyche.

Mysticism or martyrdom? There are Christ-like qualities to the 33s who sacrifice themselves for the sake of others, yet I've also known alcoholics and compulsive gamblers who carried this Master Number. Sensitive, sympathetic, and tenderhearted, they are prone to despair, carrying deep wounds within and feeling global pain. To survive the extreme emotional stress they undergo in order to achieve the Soul qualities which result from this suffering, it helps to know that the way we deal with challenges sets a great example for others. They may be an example of exactingly high idealism to which others are drawn, or they may manifest negatively in traits which others instinctively shun. Sacrifice can come in many forms. In other words, one way to serve is by being a bad example.

The premise for Master Number 33 is: 3 + 3 = 6. 3 is the artist, sculptor, aesthetic, self-expression. 6 is the server of family or community. Key Words for 33 are: Self-Awareness Through Selfless Service.

BIRTH PATH 33

Your purpose in life is to serve the needs of humanity, and your noble ideals and highly developed spiritual consciousness sweep you into the mainstream of world or community responsibility. Your prime directive is to benefit, serve, help, and minister to as many people as possible. You firmly believe in and work towards the establishment and maintenance of justice and human rights.

Steady and dependable, your strongest desire is to shield and nurture others. Love and forgiveness spring eternally and unquenchably from your heart. Your greatest rewards come from using your powers to raise the consciousness of others. You show people how to live in the world yet still have an understanding and practical use of spiritual principles, and you answer needs wherever you find them.

Love of humanity always comes first for you. You feel the concerns of family and the immediate community rather impersonally. Your foremost desire is to raise existing standards. Race, gender, or creed merit no consideration because you work and live for the good of all. You will never be idle, since your services are always in demand and your need to serve makes you want to be up and doing. Your life is happy, fulfilled, and blessed. (10, 11)

Life's Lessons for Birth Path 33

If you could take the whole world under your wing, you would do it, but failing that you find yourself active in community and civic affairs, heading charities that serve the homeless, the destitute, the hungry, and the sick, and action programs such as prison reforms or political lobbying for the underdog. You find deep satisfaction in activities which challenge rigid values, thinking, concepts, and dogmas. (8)

Like a Mother Teresa, you are capable of putting the needs of others, needs which involve empathy, love, and forgiveness, before your own desires. Your family may require attention that stretches your physical and emotional capability to the limit, sometimes without adequate emotional or financial compensation.

You may have trouble distinguishing fact from fiction when you hear someone's story of trial, so take care that requests for your services are truly needed, and not merely someone's self-centered or weak desire to avoid their own strengthening processes. You cannot be all things to all people, so be discreet with your energies or they will be spent without results. (11)

Though many responsibilities may come your way, your faith and determination are equal to the task. Don't expect to get your rewards from the people that you help. More frequently your returns will come in strange and unexpected ways. Be steadfast when the cause is just and right, and the laws of Karma will be fulfilled.

You must have a supreme realization of what Life really is in order to develop an understanding of and a reliance upon the Divine guidance within. If you live up to your inherent power, you'll be the finest example of what is possible for humans to achieve and of what abilities follow the full awakening of Self. (9, 11)

VOWEL TOTAL 33

The foundation of your heart's desire is beauty, kindness, generosity, harmony, love, peace, and truth. Though your personal actions tend to be conventional, you are broadminded, tolerant, and understanding. You respond well to responsibility, with a keen sense of duty and justice. Most of all you want to be of service to others as a sort of Cosmic Parent or Guardian. A good counselor, a sympathetic and loyal friend, your strong humanitarian instincts make you a refuge and sanctuary for those who need comforting. People bring their troubles to you, and your heart responds with a desire to right all wrongs and to lift everybody's life to a higher sense of love and service. (1)

Through love and example you show others how to make spiritual truths work in the material world by revealing the ideals that come from the depths of your understanding and knowledge. Working and associating with others is vitally necessary to you, for you could never be happy working alone. You make friends easily and are a good judge of character unless your emotions get involved. Those near and dear to you claim your fondest attentions, but from the center of your world you work for the good of all humankind. If you accept what comes your way with easy grace and live for the uplifting of others, you'll find that you, in turn, are always taken care of and protected. (1,9)

Helping Yourself with Vowel Total 33

Although your manner is usually humble and unaffected, there are those who instinctively perceive the light within you, and they will gladly follow you. So, do not hide your light, but let it shine brightly for those waiting to be shown the way. (9)

Some people will have difficulty understanding your faith and way of perceiving and living life because the harmony and good you see in all things is beyond their experience. You can find Divine order where others recognize only discord and evil. You are Love personified. Though you have a deep understanding of spiritual principles, you search constantly to find better ways to simplify the Truth so that the average consciousness can also comprehend it. There are abilities available to you that most others cannot even dream of. You don't need to preach; you demonstrate how to live in a spiritually rewarding way. Others either love you deeply because you shed light on their path or hate you fiercely because your life reveals to them their own shortcomings. People are apt to shun that which makes them feel inferior. (9)

Faith in your Soul's guidance and a compassionate heart will make your path more rewarding. To recognize and to communicate with the Soul Self is the highest path anyone can take, and it brings power and true selflessness. Your primary goal is to come to an understanding of the laws that govern this power and the lessons of its use. At the end of your life, if you've reached your goal, you will be able to demonstrate the truth of your knowledge.

CONSONANT TOTAL 33

You have a special mission in life and it may require self-sacrifice or even martyrdom, but you accept this responsibility with an unfaltering faith and belief in the ultimate good resulting from all situations. You seek active community involvement, to become a part of social service and reform, to oil the wheels of justice and right the inequities of life. Any project that promotes the betterment of humanity will have your undivided support. You do not seek fame or fortune, but satisfying results from your labors bring you deep contentment. The extent of your good works may not be recognized during your lifetime but instead may be honored posthumously.

Your life and your home reflect elegance and refinement. You are modest, patient, and forbearing, and finding your way to people and places where you can help the most comes as naturally as breathing. People from all walks of life draw deeply upon your compassion. No one is too high or too low for you to offer yourself as counselor, friend, and protector. You tolerate their idiosyncrasies and find excuses for their weaknesses. Children and animals bring out your utmost compassion.

Your life's energies are devoted to understanding and applying spiritual principles to all your activities. With all your heart you want the world to become a kinder, more loving place, and you work to bring about harmony. Others are heartened by your courage and endurance and are inspired to apply your principles to their own lives. You accept the trials of life with easy-going tolerance. You are sublimely happy when people listen to your philosophy of life and your ideals for a better society. Freedom of soul and spirit are the very essence of growth for you, and your highest joy is to bring this experience to others. (9)

Though you spend your life energies ministering to others, things of nature and loveliness bring you peace and contentment. You have difficulty adjusting to the ways of the commercial and materialistic world. Solitude brings you comfort and the solace of your inner wisdom, patience, and faith. You have a deep knowledge that your mission will be fulfilled, and inner harmony and peace are the natural result of it. Your manner is quiet and reserved, your conduct decorous and cultured. (2, 9)

The Negative Side of Consonant Total 33

Failure to live up to the high standards life demands can leave emotional scars in your psyche, and you can become worried, apprehensive and hesitant. Your stability vanishes and you retreat under criticism. You can lose perspective and martyr yourself for unworthy causes. Helping others will still be the major role of your life, but you will lack appreciation and commendation. You have fun being a trouble-shooter, and trying to make things right for those who need or ask your help takes top priority on your agenda. If you cannot find the special mission for which you are incarnated, you will suffer unhappiness and frustration.

However, it is essential to your peace of mind to develop a detachment from your sensitivity to the troubles of others, and to discover that some people are happy in their whining discontent. Allow them their right to be so, or your attempts to help will fall on infertile ground. Use your natural wisdom to understand when enough is enough. Instead of giving loaves of bread, teach others how to sow their own fields and reap their own harvests. Develop a sense of humor. Learn to laugh at your mistakes.

FULL NAME 33

You are a citizen of the Universe and your continuing mission is to develop Cosmic Consciousness and to raise the consciousness of others. Selfless service to humanity is your pathway. This number is found in Souls whose experiences have given them noble character, understanding, and compassion. This is a vibration of high tension and great power, difficult to live up to because it requires such denial of self. Your kind of courage and steadfastness of purpose would permit you to die for what you believe and find glory in the sacrifice. The mystical side of your nature is your guidance and what you feel is right directs your activities. You have little concern for what others might think. (11)

The light of your inner wisdom is a strong, attractive power, and when you speak, others find within themselves the understanding to carry on. Your speech is normally quiet and careful, but people recognize the authority that comes from true inner knowledge. The humility that naturally surrounds you brings more respect than the power you use so easily. You radiate unconditional love, good will, and protective nurturing to fellow beings in all of the physical and spiritual kingdoms of earth. In return, this concern for others creates an outpouring of love for you from those whose lives you touch. (9)

If you do not live up to your best self as a Master Number 33, you will drop to the level of a 6. You will still be called upon to serve others, but a martyr complex may be the result and you may feel that your services are useless and unappreciated.

Your experiences in this incarnation create giant steps of growth within your Soul. Teaching and setting an example are your most important roles in life. How you make a living in the physical world shouldn't trouble you; you will never be in want. (9)

Opportunities for Full Name 33

Projects dealing with children, education, the elderly, or the helpless will attract and hold your attention. No occupation or profession that is inherently destructive could ever attract you. A place in medicine or healing could channel your need to ease the suffering of others, or some field of law might serve as a way to bring justice to the downtrodden. Serving as a minister or priest could fulfill your dreams of saving others. Your gifts may also be found in the arts, where you can promote beauty, harmony, and education.

You function well in any responsible position. Loving service and patient understanding are the qualifications you bring to the job. Your sense of loyalty and civic duty could be used to advantage in educational and community projects. You have strong musical and artistic urges, and recognition may come to you as an artist or in some field of musical expression. You would do well in activities which call for vocal expression through counseling or training, or where your sense of responsibility is enhanced by your charming ability to get along with people and to win their confidence. You could become a counselor focusing on family or relationship problems. (10)

POSSIBLE VOCATIONS FOR 33

You could become an adjuster, advertiser, analyst, animal handler or trainer, anthropologist, attorney, author, cartoonist, chemist, columnist, comedian, composer, conservationist, correspondent, cosmetician, costume designer, dancer, dean, dentist, dietitian, diplomat, director of youth groups, doctor, draftsman, dramatic actor or actress, editor, educator, engineer, evangelist, executive or head of charitable organization, farmer, fashion designer, florist, foster parent, furniture dealer, gardener, geographer, gourmet cook, hairstylist, healer, herbalist, historian, home builder, homemaker, horticulturist, humorist, illustrator, industrial designer, insurance agent, journalist, lecturer, librarian, linguist, magician; manager or owner of apartments, children's home or hospital, convalescent hospital, hotel, or rest home;

manager or owner of an art store, delicatessen, gift shop, grocery store, health food store, cafe, or resort; mediator, medical researcher, metaphysician, minister, nursery school owner or worker, opera singer, painter, personnel director, pharmacist, philanthropist, philosopher, photographer, pilot, playwright, politician, portrait painter, priest, professor, psychiatrist, psychic, public service employee, publisher, radio or television personality, ranger, receptionist, sales person of beneficial products, school principal, scout troop leader, sculptor, social director, sociologist, song writer, sports director, steward or stewardess, student advisor, supervisor, surgeon, therapist, tour guide, translator, tutor, union official, veterinarian, waiter or waitress. (12)

7

===

44—PHILANTHROPIST OR DESPOT?

"It's not the money that counts, it's what you can do with the money," said Joyce, whose Vowel Total 44 has taught her discipline in finances. "Money is a tool, not an end in itself. Given a goal to strive for, money, people, and materials come easily to achieve that goal."

44s are found in the arenas of world welfare, providing jobs for the jobless, food for the hungry, homes for the homeless. They are Masters of the material, but their pathway is not an easy one because they must work against the inertia of less aware people. Their rewards may be in accomplishment and recognition as often as money.

They are apt to be conservative and do not flaunt their gifts. Much of their work may be done in secret or behind the scenes, while others take the credit. They could even head secret philanthropies, helping others through anonymous donations or using a fictitious name.

The Soul's demand of the holder of the Master Number 44 is to develop the self-control and perseverance needed to organize time and talents in order to make the best spiritual use of the material good that comes so naturally to them. Expansion of consciousness comes about through the experiences we create for ourselves on the earth plane, and if the seeker wants to reach a goal, time, patience, and discipline are necessary ingredients.

44s are quick to assure us that living well is not unspiritual. The power in this number can bring either mind-boggling success or forlorn failure, but the choice is conscious. If they ignore the higher aspirations of the Soul and yield to intolerance, love of power, and self-centeredness, they can rise to great heights by trampling on others, becoming egocentric dictators. Or, because of fear, they can abdicate their larger possibilities and become workaholics in minor positions or restrict their activities to lording it over the home base. (3)

The premise for Master Number 44: 4 + 4 = 8. 4 is the worker, duty-bound, steadfast. 8 is the manager of money, time, resources, talents. Key Words for 44 are: Self-Mastery Through Self-Discipline.

BIRTH PATH 44

This Master Number brings strength and the ability to achieve full mental discipline over mind and body. It requires self-control in all areas of living in order to fulfill your spiritual goal of furthering material good for humanity. You are particularly useful in activities that ease the physical stresses and problems of others. You have a keen mentality but may need to develop the intuitive side of your nature to discern between true needs and unwillingness to take on responsibilities when others bring their problems to you. So many people respond to your willingness to help that you feel pulled in many directions. Take time out to keep your affairs in order, so that you don't neglect your own growth for others.

Your greatest desire should be to improve all phases of life, so direct your efforts towards a goal or purpose that will benefit large numbers of people. If you broaden your viewpoint beyond the personal, you will discover that for you there are no limitations. You have a talent to arouse others to greater effort, to achieve their own successes. You show by example how to make business profitable, yet honest and ethical, and how to do things for the world in a dramatic and effective way. You are a very good person to have in any alliance, business, marriage, or other partnership. Still, you remain choosy in your personal relationships. (3, 6)

With a natural ability to judge character and a philosophical turn of mind, you have a sympathetic understanding of human nature that allows you to overlook most of its frailties. You have the ability to master great challenges which will give you the wise judgment that Life demands of you. Your most satisfying accomplishments will come about when you apply spiritual wisdom to making money. Be generous. Give as you would receive. You should be philanthropic, altruistic, well-balanced, and just. Base your decisions on common sense and logic. Prosperity and economic progress are your birthright—used wisely together, they make your life happy and fulfilled. (2, 3, 4, 7)

Order and stability are vital ingredients for your happiness. If you have a negative side, it may manifest as inflexibility, stubbornness, dogmatism, and insensitivity; or you may have a love of power, be domineering, scheming, boastful, greedy, impatient, dictatorial, cruel, vengeful, or unreasonable. You have a conservative approach to life, and fear of making a bad judgment may make you too conventional and restrict your creativity. Work to cultivate your courage for freedom of action so that you maintain a free flow of intuition that is so vital to your Soul growth. (3)

Life's Lessons for Birth Path 44

In past lives you have gained much power, sometimes through ruthless means. This is the lifetime to balance this Karma by putting your dynamic energy to work for the world's underprivileged. You have great vigor and stamina and, to get the most out of your capabilities, you must learn to efficiently manage your energy, time, and money. (2)

You need to know about the laws of money and other assets, and the laws of the business and commercial world. They govern the large sums you must be prepared to handle if you want to succeed in your Life's purpose. Use all of your abilities to aid you in fulfilling your destiny, but be careful not to land in the pit of desiring self-gain. Self-centered use of your energies will always negate the larger things you are capable of achieving. (1, 9)

You will utilize spiritual energies more effectively for material success when you realize that this power always works best when used to advance humanity as a whole. Greater achievements and acclaim can be won through groups and organizations where you add your energy to that of others who have similar aims and purposes. Strive to associate with people of wealth or authority, to work in harmony with philanthropic groups, private enterprises with large visions, or governmental programs. Look for opportunities to build something of lasting benefit to yourself and humanity. Teach others from your own insights and inspirations. If you have the education and the background for it, a political career or international work could provide the stage on which to make your great ideals known to more people. (1, 7, 9)

VOWEL TOTAL 44

Your Heart's Desire is to make spiritual issues practical in keeping with your deep beliefs as to how this world should be. To bring universal concepts into physical being, you are willing to battle overwhelming odds, if by doing so you can aid in the advancement of world concerns. You make a great mediator because you have the ability to calm troubled emotions using your great resourcefulness, logic and common sense to solve everyday problems.

In this incarnation you will develop both mind and body. Physical and mental stamina are your personal pride. You have a wholesome view of life and are conscientious and ethical in all that you do. Straight-shooting and sincere in your motives, there is a fine balance of orderliness in your nature. You dislike pettiness and have great integrity and self-respect. You keep your promises, and you are often disappointed that everyone else does not live up to the high-principled guidelines you set for yourself. You steer clear of the shallowness of most social relationships, preferring deeper and more intimate affiliations with family and a few trusted and loyal friends. Always very punctual, you hate to be kept waiting, and you have a genuine aversion to things left unfinished or done inaccurately. A strict sense of duty and obligation pushes you to reach your goals in life, and your successes benefit not only yourself but your loved ones and your community. (5, 6, 9, 11)

Although you strive for respectability and stability, you can also attract power, recognition, status, and the best in everything because you are systematic, open-handed, large-minded, and trustworthy. Your loyalty and reliability are guideposts to others. They feel secure in knowing your position on all issues and are confident that you will treat all personal and business transactions honestly and fairly. (2, 3)

In business or family relationships, your natural demeanor is serious and practical. To find someone who can give genuine help in producing real and tangible results from your ideas, look for a business or love partner whose perspective is also practical. The foundations of your life must be stable and secure, and there must be a goal towards which you are striving or you tend to become melancholy, anxious, and restless. (6)

Helping Yourself with Vowel Total 44

Your Soul Self has the secret. It has mastered many virtues, but the purpose of this incarnation is to learn how to make your spiritual powers useful on the material plane. If you allow it, your Soul Self will bring areas and projects to your attention that will develop your great potentials. Don't work only for personal aims, but choose worthy and far-reaching goals, and your courage and energy will escalate you to a high position in your chosen field. (6)

You are happiest in activities that work towards concrete results rather than philosophical ones. You are a reliable worker, a powerhouse full of energy and resolve. Exercising discipline allows you to maintain steady progress toward your goal and to eventually succeed.

You have latent ability to understand and to work with psychological principles, and you might find research in this field rewarding. Misdirected, this energy might lead to personal biases that could undermine any real success in life. You want and need the respect and support of those around you, which prejudice, rebellion, or jealousy can destroy. Develop an impersonal overview of life and an unconditional love for others. Self-discipline will bring you opportunities to supervise and command without overtones of self-righteousness. (5, 6)

Your stick-to-itiveness is an asset. It enables you to overcome obstacles and to get decisive results. Sometimes you get hung up with details and become annoyed if little things go wrong or are left unattended; this comes from your deep conscientiousness. But, be easier on yourself and others. To get too involved in details can cause you to overlook the larger picture. Never lose sight of the fact that the possessor of a Master Number has greater abilities, greater responsibilities, and greater powers of self-mastery. Life expects more from you and you have the ability to live up to those expectations. Don't be an ostrich. You are destined for greater things. (6)

Watch out for the tendency to ride roughshod over the suggestions of others. Your capabilities and ideas are top-notch, but you raise yourself in the esteem of your family and fellow workers and receive more cooperation when you recognize and put to use their good ideas too. Don't let your busy mind become so preoccupied that others think of you as abrupt and unfeeling. Your natural diplomacy and tact will always smooth troubled waters. (11)

CONSONANT TOTAL 44

In appearance you are commanding and masterful, with an aura of success and prosperity. You are equally at home in the world of finance, on a board of directors, or as the president of a large organization or company, perhaps your own. You are good at organizing, directing, planning, supervising, handling large amounts of money—controlling the flow of enterprise and the activities of many employees. You are respected and admired, and you make a good boss or supervisor, but you expect much from people, sometimes more than they are capable of giving. (1, 5, 9, 11)

A natural administrator, you have a talent for organizing people and activities without bossiness or fanfare. Impartial, honest, and forthright, your fire and zeal are contagious and inspiring, spurring others on to their own success and happiness. (11)

Purpose and planning are strong characteristics in all that you do, but if you are too earthy you may become too materialistic and lose your high spirituality. Because you want to accomplish so much, you could overextend your energies and suffer health consequences. It is necessary for your well-being to make yourself slow down and relax, to approach life with less intensity. (11)

At your best, you are sincere, straightforward, capable, dependable, and generous, with great leadership and organizational abilities and the desire to render practical service. Responsibility, integrity, and honor are your finest characteristics. You move with an air of authority and have ambition and personal magnetism. Endowed with patience, persistence, and strength of character, you have the courage and willpower to keep trying until you achieve what you set out to do. These attributes should give you prestige, position, and power among family and friends and in the workplace. (2, 3)

Strong protective forces embrace you, and you draw from an enormous wellspring of inner strength. You are spirited and brave—sometimes to the point of foolhardiness. You are at peace with your thoughts and yourself, and you can be alone without being lonely. (2, 11)

The Negative Side of Consonant Total 44

If you allow yourself to misuse the power you hold, you could become sly and greedy, seeking personal aggrandizement rather than general good. If you lose perspective and allow yourself to become secretive, vengeful and cruel, you could divert the flow of money into your own coffers instead of the rightful use for which it was intended. If your desire for worldly goods and status becomes too unrealistic for your education and background, it can lead to overexertion, accidents, illness, and general breakdown. Keep on the alert for new chances to enhance your education. Allow unexpected happenings to broaden your horizons and increase your understanding.

Discouragement can give rise to violent and disruptive energies from the negative side of your nature, which can affect others as well as yourself. Guard against becoming self-centered, fault-finding, dictatorial, obstinate, crude, complaining, or unreasonable. Remember that anger, jealousy, and other negative emotions can destroy others as easily as can acts of violence.

If you become so materialistic that duty, drudgery, and toil take all of your energy, you'll lose contact with the aims and goals of the Soul Self and your Master powers will deteriorate. Realize that all things have a spiritual counterpoint, and try to bring balance to the material and the spiritual.

FULL NAME 44

It cannot be repeated too often that developing self-discipline is your spiritual purpose in life, and all of your experiences will serve to bring this about. The purpose of this incarnation is to gain mastery over all areas of your life, and self-knowledge is the key to this fulfillment. Philosophical, mystical, and religious areas of thought will provide guidelines to expand your mental and spiritual understanding. (2, 6)

You have good physical, mental, and emotional development, but you may need to develop more fully the intuitional side of your nature as the next step in spiritual growth. Become more alert to hunches and the workings of your inner mind. The Soul Self has more knowledge of the unseen side of life than your personality may be currently expressing. Make it an objective to listen more intently to inner promptings and use them to serve the physical needs of humanity through solid, efficient, and productive activities. Recognize that the really first-class ideas you have come from the inner Self and use them to build for posterity as well as prosperity. Your work may very well out-live you, especially in areas of social reform.

Your energy is best used to make the world a better place physically. You have the inventiveness to accomplish this. You are not a spendthrift, but can be generous with those you love as well as with charitable, philanthropic, and religious organizations. (2)

You are meticulous, systematic, sincere, loyal, impartial, and just. Order, symmetry, and method regulate the work you do, and you radiate power and authority as the well-organized business executive. The qualities of stamina, determination, reliability, and straightforward practicality take you far on the road to success. Your air of confidence, efficiency, and strength causes others to seek you out for leadership. Intense concentration and strong willpower stand you in good stead in emergencies and you are able to treat difficult situations in a calm and easy manner. (3, 9)

Yours is an outstanding destiny, with dynamic energies that you can direct into wealth, acclaim, and status. All this comes easier to you when material and spiritual energies have been blended, and you learn to consider what is the best for everyone involved rather than working for personal aims alone. Your greatest fulfillment comes as you apply beauty of character and self-mastery to enterprise and persistence, but the love and satisfaction of accomplishment must outstrip your desire for personal praise. Life does not end with the attainment of one goal, but true achievement comes from building on past successes, one upon another. No one remains static in the world. If you do not progress, you must regress. Your future is assured if your visions encompass mighty goals. (6)

If you do not live up to your best self, position and wealth can lead to greed and ruthlessness. Then you will find restrictions on all sides and your dreams will go unfulfilled. Rebelling against the constraints will bring about attitudes of envy, petulance, or narrow-mindedness, and your life will be filled with small tasks and small rewards. (2, 5)

You will always be in the winner's seat if you keep your breadth of viewpoint and admit to no limitation. Accept with graciousness and discrimination the high position your name can create for you. Use the law of correspondences—act as you would become. Living as a great person will make you a great person. Devote your energy to the ideals within your highest aspirations, live by your natural optimism and peace of mind. Satisfaction and tremendous works will be the natural result. (1, 2)

Opportunities for Full Name 44

Your life work must be based upon service and dedicated to the progress of humanity. Occupations that require accuracy, concentration, and steadfastness fit your talents. You have a great deal of stamina and you are not afraid of hard work. You enjoy working in areas that create permanent and lasting results, with physical and tangible objectives. (5)

A position of manager, organizer, or administrator of some practical program will use your talents fully. Even if you work in education, politics, religion, or another rather abstract field, you get great satisfaction from organizing facts and data. A good planner, you know how to handle power and how to create dreams and make them come true. Analytical, thrifty, conscientious, and dependable, your judgment is sound and your dealings are honest, fair, and wise. Progress and activity bring out the best in you because you expect, work for, and get big results. (6, 11)

The kinds of occupations in which you could find your niche are many and varied. You will always exert power and influence over those around you, no matter where you go or what you do. (11)

POSSIBLE VOCATIONS FOR 44

Administrator, advertiser; anything in the financial world; anthropologist, architect, athlete, attorney, author, builder, band or orchestra leader, botanist, business analyst; character analyst, chiropodist, chiropractor, civil servant, coach, commercial artist, corporate executive, critic, dentist, detective, doctor, draftsman, ecologist, editor, educator, efficiency expert, electrical engineer, employment agent, engineer, entrepreneur, estate manager, explorer, fundraiser, gardener, genealogist, geographer, head of a school, importer/exporter, insurance agent, investigator, judge, landscaper, logistics expert, manager, master mechanic, mathematician, merchant, military officer, news anchor or reporter, office manager, osteopath, personnel director, philanthropist, physicist, pilot, printer, probation officer, public official, publisher, purchasing agent; rancher, real estate agent or broker, researcher, retailer, sales manager, salesperson, sculptor, skilled craftsman, welfare worker, supervisor, veterinarian, vocational counselor. (12)

8

====

55—FREQUENT FLYER
OR LOCAL COMMUTER?

"How can I soar like an eagle when I have to work with turkeys?" Jereme, tired of buzzing around the room, his favorite airplane making loops and dips, had flopped on his back in the middle of the rug, still flying his plane at arm's length.

Of course! Jereme, in his play, was only parroting the adults laughing about a bumper sticker, but the similarity to the Master Number 55 struck me as hilariously funny.

55 expresses the spiritual evolution of the Number 1 vibration. While the 1 struggles to find his or her identity, the 5 shouts it aloud to the world: "I am ME, the one and only." Both numbers express independence, acting from the "I want to know" standpoint; both express curiosity mixed with derring-do.

The Soul's demand of the holder of the Master Number 55 is to integrate the mind and Soul which act together for the expansion of human mentality. Both the 5 and the 1 are generally nonconformists in their approach to life, and bonded together they can create an increase in spiritual consciousness that brings forth new forms of thought and action to pave the way for innovative spiritual insight. The experiences created act as catalysts for further growth. Faith Javane writes about the ability of 55 in her book *Master Numbers, Cycles of Divine Order*, "From new patterns of thought...will come the ability for mental telepathy, healing, astral projection, clairvoyance and prophecy..."

Soul memories of past experiences create inner wisdom and an instinctive knowledge of the right approach to any situation. If past-life experiences have been painful and lessons have been learned through severe repercussions, unrecognized fear may be present in the inner Self. The individual then may stifle the desire to reach out for new experience, and may lose opportunities for further spiritual insight along this Path. If because of fear (or Karma—which often manifests as a missing 1), the holder of a 55 doesn't recognize or is afraid to accept the adventures presented, they will spend their days commuting to and from work. The Number 1 influence gives them a solid foundation to become successful in business, or to find adventure in far lands, either physically or mentally, but they may choose not to accept these opportunities to "soar with eagles."

The premise for Master Number 55 is: $5 + 5 = 10 = 1$. 1 is the individualist, pioneer, loner. 5 is the traveler, globe-trotter, loves experience. Key Words for 55 are: Self-Development Through Self-Knowledge.

BIRTH PATH 55

You are progressive, independent, generous, but you must be in the driver's seat, for you have too much savvy to serve elsewhere. A born leader, innovator, and planner, you do not hesitate to take on the unusual or original. Your qualities of strength, willpower, and courage create a very positive nature. An independent thinker and frequently a nonconformist in thought and action, you are unhappy if life denies you the right to follow your own ideas and convictions. You do your best work when free to follow your own mental paths, and quickly lose your eagerness and animation when roadblocks are placed on your creativity. (2, 4, 6)

Inclined to be egocentric, you work best alone, or with special interest groups whose aims parallel your own. Impatience with ineptitude and lack of vision in others frustrates you. Life should be fascinating if you make the most of your gumption, inspiration, and originality. Your broad vision, magnetic personality, and adventurous mind will carry you into challenging work experiences and into the lives of interesting people, who help you fulfill your plans and make your dreams financially rewarding. (3, 6)

An energetic activist, an avid reader, and a clever and fluent talker with a keen sense of humor, you bring sparkle to any group. Although you love and empathize with people as a whole, you possess a deep inner sensitivity; you form very few close relationships, losing interest in those who cannot keep up with your facile and constantly searching mind. Long-lasting marriage ties may not be for you, unless the 1 in your Birth Path is stronger than the 5. (3)

You have a strong interest in what is going on around you, and you are in top form if you can have more than one activity going at a time. However, you are apt to become restless and impatient if results come too slowly or you find yourself stuck in boring and repetitive situations. You are a quick, imaginative thinker, and have no trouble keeping up with fast-moving activities. You can become expert in any enterprise or business line that is progressive. When sufficiently aroused, you allow no obstacle to stand in your way. You can be very analytical, too, and get a kick out of stirring things up when you think people are becoming too pompous or didactic; but the up side of your nature is benevolent, tolerant, and helpful. (6)

If you manifest the obverse forms of these qualities, you can become domineering and indiscreet. You may become dictatorial and obstinate if you feel your freedom to act or think is limited or ordered by others. If freedom is denied you for too long a time, you may lose confidence in yourself and become indecisive. (2)

Since all experiences are yours for the asking, you must be careful not to overindulge in addictive activities such as gambling, food, drink, tobacco, sex, drugs, or other pleasure stimulants; you could easily exhaust your body and waste your talents. Your strong will can help you minimize these activities. In some cases you should avoid them entirely, because "kicking the habit" is more difficult for you than for most people. Realizing that you may have what is termed an "addictive nature" gives you power to take charge of your own life and its purposes. (4, 6)

Life's Lessons for Birth Path 55

The art of happiness and the full expression of your individuality is the goal of this Birth Path. You must become aware and in control of your own self-reliant powers, and turn your attention to using them for the benefit of humanity. Your lifelong challenge will be to learn the right use of willpower—how it can be used to fulfill your wishes, but not at the expense of the rights of others. (2, 9)

The full range and individuality of your body, mind, and spirit must be developed if you want to realize your highest destiny. Endowed with executive ability, keen perception, good concentration and a broad vision, you can direct the undertakings of others or establish your own enterprises. Carefully continue to strengthen and perfect your powers to lead, control, and coordinate in this lifetime as you progress toward your spiritual goal of responsibility in leadership. (1, 4, 6, 9)

Accept the challenge to lead, but choose helpers whose talents make them good assistants, and then be sure to let them know how much you appreciate them. If you seek them out, you can meet intelligent, progressive, scientific, inventive, and resourceful people who will value your good qualities and help you to achieve your goals. (1, 7, 9)

Adventure—more varied types of experience than most people will know—can be the keynote of your life. Your mercurial nature may make you inconsistent, expressing one thing today, another tomorrow. This quality can be exploited by using your versatility to change with the times and to keep up with the progress of the world. Doing more than one thing at a time will not tax your inexhaustible energies. Learn to use your native ingenuity to solve problems that arise, and let your ever-present sense of humor and mental resilience help you when facing opposition. (2, 7)

VOWEL TOTAL 55

Your heart's desire is to march at the head of the parade, to be the authoritative figure in any circumstance in which you find yourself—to be the promoter or director. Taking a lesser position dulls your willingness to participate or use your vast skills to the utmost. You make a better employer than employee because you'd rather work alone or be in charge of situations where everything is done your way. Detail work bores you, and you may ignore it or leave it to others while you spend your attention on more interesting and challenging aspects of the job. (2, 5, 9)

Free-thinking and independent, you claim complete and total freedom as your personal heritage. You allow others the right to follow their own visions and to live their own lives, and you demand the same rights for yourself. Very ambitious, your strength of character and mental agility help you to get ahead in the world. Intense, honest, loyal, and driven, you are resolute in your desire to succeed in whatever you set yourself to do. Those qualities of leadership such as bravery in the face of discouragement, determination, and reliance upon inner resources give you the will to do and to achieve. You are strongly individualized and vital, and if you use your creative and practical ideas in helpful and constructive ways, you'll find you can be a leader in your profession or work. (2, 3, 6)

If your life is lived on the positive side, you will manifest unselfishness and strong spiritual ideals. Your mental processes are direct and keen, and your thoughts are always progressive and optimistic. You have a pioneering spirit, pushing continually forward, and can be active, bold, and forceful. You have no trouble standing alone when the going gets tough, and others find in you a bastion of strength and courage when their own lives are turbulent. (4, 9, 11)

You are clever, versatile, and intensely interested in activities where repartee and wit put you in the limelight. Your great personal magnetism injects new life into whatever you touch, so that wherever you go you create a spark of energy. You're naturally the center of attention in any group, even if you interact only briefly. You are often the subject of publicity, even when you do not seek it. (2, 3, 9)

Helping Yourself with Vowel Total 55

Often willful and impetuous, you don't like to take orders or be told what to do. You want to see results quickly and are often impatient with slower minds and the need to wait while manifestation (which is slower in coming than your ideas) catches up with the impetus to begin new projects. Thus you sometimes appear perverse, domineering, or egotistical, and this can build up to misunderstanding and arguments. (6)

You have an excellent memory, but on the other side of the coin, you find it difficult to release resentment and old grudges. When you must work with others, the sterling qualities of courage, strong will, and the ability to triumph over hardships may develop negatively into an unpleasant, dominating attitude of superiority. You could become conceited, arrogant, critical, and impatient. A genuine, sincere interest in other people and their problems and goals will help you realign such negative traits. People respond to your positive characteristics and delight in helping you. Your life should be interesting and fun. (2, 3, 4, 11)

Wherever you go, you feel you should be accepted as the natural leader of whatever is going on, and so you will be, as long as you remain kind and thoughtful of others. Stand up for your rights, keep your emotional balance, and maintain confidence in yourself and pride in your achievements. But remember to respect others' need to feel important too, and present your ideas and plans with graciousness, generosity, and sincerity. Then people will accept you as a respected and capable leader. (6)

If you have a tendency toward mental rather than physical work, you will have a deep interest in scientific study and research. You could make an excellent writer because you think innovatively and challenge stereotypes. You adapt easily to new people and situations, but if you find yourself in a routine job or environment and you work with the same people every day, you will soon stagnate and lose vitality. You desire to be a part of what is going on around you, so groups or public activity can open avenues through which to achieve your goals. Your life will always be filled with action and many different kinds of experiences. You accept change easily, instinctively knowing that while not all change is progress, all progress is change. (6, 8, 11)

Freedom and liberty are vital to your good health, and travel is a natural revitalizer. "A change in occupation is as good as a vacation," says an old adage. When you begin to get restless, frustrated, or inattentive, do something different to release the tension. Buy a new outfit, go on a trip (even if it's only a Sunday jaunt), or make some positive change in your work or home life. Freedom means you don't have to live in a rut, bound to routine and duty. You can, and should, live a rich, full life and inspire others to follow your lead. Value your ingenuity; use it to make your life more productive and to bring happiness to those around you. (6, 8)

CONSONANT TOTAL 55

You take great pleasure in the activities of living. Your experiences encompass adventures in both the external world and in your own internal world, and you respond with energy and daring. You are excited by new challenges and the possibility of adventure, becoming bored easily by repeated situations and routine activities. You prefer physical experiences, wanting to learn firsthand about all the phases of living. The sense of freedom and detachment gained from many such encounters makes you multifaceted, liberal, and tolerant, with an expanded viewpoint and depth of Being. (3, 5)

Vitally interested in new people, places and activities, you are also discerning, investigative, and communicative. Your excellent reasoning power makes you well-equipped to examine any proposal or item and to report your findings either verbally or in writing. You live enthusiastically and can react with intense emotionalism to unexpected situations. You have the ability to separate the wheat from the chaff and can present the truth carefully and clearly when necessary. You are not prone to flattery or superficialities. Generous, tolerant and unselfish, you can be trusted to never betray a confidence. (11)

Your speech and actions are direct and sincere. You are an

imaginative and independent thinker with a fine sense of humor; you do not bend easily to authority or tradition and are not easily influenced by the opinions of others. Once you make a decision, it's full speed ahead, and you allow no obstacle to stand in your way. It doesn't bother you if others cannot keep up or aren't willing to go where you are headed. They can stay behind for all you care. You are quite content to work alone. (2, 3, 5)

Freedom of thought and action is essential for you. Advancements are made through the wisdom that comes with trial and error, so you have the courage to reclaim your mistakes, ambition for success, and willingness to let go of the safe to experiment with the untried. The ideal use of your capabilities is to defend the rights of others to express their uniqueness. Your purpose and delight is to show (as well as teach) people how to live more fulfilled and happy lives; you know by experience that lasting happiness cannot exist when one is restricted or bound by people or circumstances. Others look up to your strength and force of character, and seek to emulate your honesty and high-mindedness. Stay attuned to the light within you and you will draw to yourself the highest quality of the things you desire. (2, 6)

Your greatest talents lie in the areas of communication and all lines of inquiry and intrigue. You are strong, brave, bold, vital, and alert—the innovator, instigator, and investigator of new plans, unusual ideas, and the strange and provocative. Use your courage, perseverance, and ambition to invent new and progressive applications of old ideas.

You are seen as unique, sometimes egocentric, sometimes a loner, but decidedly different. People respect and listen to you because you go directly to the heart of the matter and can quickly evaluate all the ramifications and potentials of any project or situation. Your leadership is accepted because you are the one who sees the work through to the end, the one whose ideas are efficient and effective. Putting dreams into action is your forte, and others are encircled and drawn along by your enthusiasm, your irresistible charm. (11)

You have a lot of pride and are easily humiliated and embarrassed. Disgrace can be devastating to you. Your tastes are definitely to the manor born and you want the people and circumstances for which you are responsible—your spouse, your children, your home, the products of your mind and hands—to reflect your own ideals of quality. (1, 3, 9)

The Negative Side of Consonant Total 55

Keep your aspirations pure because dreams of self-aggrandizement can make you boastful, contemptuous of others and their opinions, headstrong, and egotistical. You can become arrogant, praise-seeking, and uncritical of flattery from others. You may refuse to take advice or to be told what to do. Self-centeredness is a definite danger and can bring on callousness, irresponsibility, irreverence, and self-indulgence. You will remain in the good graces of your friends and secure in leadership as long as you follow the charitable urges of your heart and remember your prime directive: all people must have the same freedom of thought and action that you demand for yourself. (2, 3, 6)

You are prone to stand by your convictions no matter who speaks against you. You have difficulty admitting you are wrong at any time—even if important relationships are disrupted by your stance. Work to guard against this trait; being able to form new opinions when divergent facts are presented to you shows the versatility of a great mind. Allow others to be right sometimes. Life designs hardships and obstacles to help you gain enlightenment and enhance the unusual qualities that are characteristic of your individuality. (11)

You love sensual pleasures and they are yours in abundance. However, you are apt to bore quickly and constantly move on to new stimulations. You may be ruled by passion or anger, and your bearing may be overly aggressive or dominating. If your aims are prompted by self-centeredness, you could become miserly, crabby, secretive, deceitful, and obstinate. Let your natural altruism, noble ideals, and spiritual aspirations be the guidelines of your life. (2, 5)

FULL NAME 55

You are versatile, smart, and courageous. Your achievements come through the force of your self-reliance and self-determination. You walk your path with pride and assurance, because you know that your highest calling is to be an example for all. You move forward quickly and you are never happy when things slow down, because your high energy level demands that you be constantly active. (8, 9)

Refuse to acknowledge limitations, but learn to cooperate without losing your self-identity. Instead of rebelling against the burdens life hands you, remember you have the ability to think freely, to create new concepts, establish new methods, and originate your own strategies. Do not limit yourself to ordinary paths, unless there is no other sensible or practical road to take. As a pioneer in interesting and unknown realms, whether commercial, artistic, philosophic, or scientific, come to your own independent conclusions. (1, 7)

If you do not live up to your best self, you manifest the characteristics of a dictator with all the unpleasant traits of aggression, dominance, and ruthlessness. Your activities may become confused and disordered. Erratic thoughts and actions will create blind alleys, alienate friends, coworkers, and even family members, and make your life barren and lonely. You'll demonstrate arrogance instead of initiative and courage, and self-centered aims will overshadow group aims. Use the energy from your Master Number 55 for honest and constructive purposes only. (2)

Ideas come faster than you can apply them, and a lack of patience in letting things manifest in their own time can create stress and destructive frustration. An explosive temper may erupt when obstacles hinder your plans. The watchwords for strong feelings are caution and restraint. (3, 5)

It disturbs you to scatter your mental forces. You work rapidly and well when not interrupted, and you resent anyone else interfering with your programs. Learning to cooperate is one of your life's toughest lessons. Even though you seem to be able to tap into an inexhaustible energy source, you should guard against physical or mental overwork. There is always tomorrow. Seek nontaxing relaxations at night, and let your brain and body rest. (7)

Opportunities for Full Name 55

You do very well in using your ingenuity to develop new plans and projects that make use of your enterprising and executive ability, but you must be allowed to carry out your ideas unhampered by tradition or the commonplace. Bold and daring, sometimes even rash, your courage will carry you far if used constructively. (1, 6, 11)

Meeting people comes easily and negotiating with several persons at the same time is no problem. You are happiest in a job that offers variety and an opportunity to use your insatiable curiosity and active mental ability. Your closest friends should be educators and philosophers, especially those in the vanguard of new thought. (5, 9)

You have an easy way with words and would make an outstanding lecturer or salesperson on the road, since you understand all the nuances of persuasion and you enjoy traveling. Communication is your forte and exchanging information with the many different types of people you meet along the way will enrich your life and enhance your knowledge. Sharing the revelations and depths of your special focus in life is a basic need and you can exploit writing and all mediums of communication to satisfy that need. You react keenly to injustices and indifference in the world—some aspect of politics or religion could fulfill your drive to express yourself on these points. You would make an excellent detective or librarian, since you love to research strange projects, unearth buried information, or piece together odd bits to form a whole picture.

In your vocational choices you have unlimited opportunity, but you will be happiest off the beaten track. Your restless nature makes it difficult to settle down to routine work. Your greatest assets are your individuality, initiative, and creative self-sufficiency, and your talents are best used in circumstances where you work by yourself or with people who follow your commands. Since you do not like to be bossed or to take orders, you could provide an individual service or be at the head of a business, maybe your own or as the head of a department. If that isn't feasible, look for a job where you can be clever, creative, original, and have the authority to make quick decisions but not be pressured. (2, 4, 6, 9)

You have a sense of drama and comedy, and some field of amusement or entertainment could develop these talents. Schools and colleges, or any kind of enterprise which is unusual or challenging, could make good use of your passion. (6)

POSSIBLE VOCATIONS FOR 55

Among other things you could be an advertiser, ambassador, analyst, architect, art or antique shop owner, artist, athletic coach, attorney, booking agent, bookstore owner, broadcaster, broker, buyer, captain, carnival worker or artist, character analyst, civil servant, claims adjuster, commercial artist, contractor, critic, dancer, dean, diagnostician, dowser, electrician, entrepreneur, fashion designer, film director, foreman, geographer, guide, humorist, inspector, interior decorator, jeweler, landscaper, manufacturer, merchant marine, messenger, minister, mountaineer, movie producer, musician, navigator, oceanographer, Peace Corps volunteer, personal consultant, personnel director, pilot, plastic surgeon, politician, private detective, producer, professional athlete, psychiatrist, psychologist, publicist, race car driver, rancher, satirist, scientist, sea captain, secret service agent, singer, specialist in internal medicine, speculator, speech writer, teacher of the occult, telephone operator, tour guide, trader, translator, travel agent, writer of mystery or detective stories; anything in communication such as author, cartoonist, correspondent, education, English or foreign language professor, illustrator, journalist, photographer, radio or television personality. (12)

9

==

66—Cosmic Consciousness or Path of Sorrow?

"Please kiss it and make it well." Jereme was trying hard not to cry as he presented his skinned elbow for my inspection. I kissed him, cleaned the dirt and blood away, and applied a bandage. As he scampered off to play again, I reflected how much easier it is to heal a physical hurt than to heal an emotional hurt.

Cosmic Consciousness is the reward and the end result of the Soul's need to attune with God, Who is not only the source of life but also the source of the permeating drive to experience all things: joy and sadness, love and hate, life and death, nurturing and destroying. Negative experiences invariably lead to positive reflections, strengthening the Soul's knowledge of correct responses, illuminating the darkness, and building a deeper desire to probe into the mysteries of life and universal truth.

The Soul's demand of the holder of Master Number 66 is for personal transformation through compassion and love. Every Soul must pass through the crucible of sorrow and pain until it learns to rightly use the laws of harmony and order: how to love and how to forgive. A test is a test until it is no longer recognized as a test. As each lesson is learned, the Soul blossoms anew into joy and graciousness, and living is directed more truly towards cooperation and goodwill, unifying all beings and restoring peace to the world. Faith Javane in *Master Numbers: Cycles of Divine Order* explains, "... [H]uman desires such as lust, greed, hate, envy, and all other attributes of the lower senses must become fully subject to the Christ within . . . . "

Master Number 66, perhaps above all others, has the capacity for a profound compassion for the distress of others, because the holder has traveled deep into the byways of sorrow. Empathetic and perhaps telepathic, 66 has a psychic sense tuned to finding, understanding, and helping to ease the emotional pain of companions along the way.

The premise for Master Number 66 is: 6 + 6 = 12 = 3. 3 is the artist, sculptor, aesthetic, self-expressionist. 6 is the server of family or community. Key Words for 66 are: Self-Expression Through Service, Harmony, and Creativity.

BIRTH PATH 66

At your best, your ideals are noble and you have great dreams for their fulfillment. Your highest desire is to help others, especially by creating and sustaining justice and human rights. You may even be a master of the lesser hierarchy walking incognito upon the earth. As such, you would throw yourself upon the altar of sacrifice for others and count the cost small. (2)

You have a loving, responsive nature—happy, kind, extroverted, and loyal. Rarely fault-finding, you make a pleasant companion and are adored by the opposite sex. Love dominates your world and your purpose in life is to teach others this concept through gracious understanding. As the artist, the ultimate self-expressionist, you possess a vivid imagination, deep wells of emotion, and fruitful inspiration. With acute intelligence you penetrate the heart of situations clearly and completely. Even though you seek pleasure as the essence of true living, you also have a deeply serious side; you understand that life can but must not be frittered away. (2, 6)

You are eloquent with words and can make this gift a financial asset. However, you need to watch your emotions—if caught off guard you'll find yourself talking too much and at the wrong time. Follow your inner hunches. Your imagination and intuition can put you in positions where you can do things on a large scale. Your creative abilities are so powerful that when used successfully, they can supply you with all that you ask from life. Your charming, easygoing disposition and an inner feeling of self-sufficiency make it possible for you to achieve magnificent accomplishments, even deeds of great courage, because you naturally gravitate to those who are in need of help. (6)

Service to others is the keynote of your life, and responsibility is the motivating force that spurs you on. Prosperity, love, friends, and admiration—most of your successes in life—come as a result of your teaching and serving, and of the generous, caring things you do for others. (6)

You may marry early. Your home and family are the center of your universe. Beauty and harmony are vital to your emotional health and these must always be in your surroundings. Your home is filled with flowers, music, and your artistic creations. The common, the crass, and the obscene are unsettling to the balance and rhythm that arise from the depths of your soul. (2)

Life's Lessons for Birth Path 66

Base your vocation on your wonderful tendency to see the good in everything and to find beauty everywhere; that is where you'll find the best opportunities to develop yourself. Your greatest rewards will be found through serving others, smoothing out altercations in home and family situations and in community activities and decisions, voluntarily giving emotional, spiritual, or material assistance where requested, working for improvements wherever needed, giving thoughtful, insightful counsel, and, in general, trying to be useful. (9)

Your ability to understand another's point of view, even a radical one, makes you a natural counselor and arbitrator when troubles come up in your business or personal life or in the lives of others. It's easy for you to find an optimistic outlook in difficult situations and to bring light and hope into the dark places of the heart. You have a knack for discovering points of harmony between divergent viewpoints and soothingly help others to meet on nonthreatening ground. You help negative thinkers see their challenges in a more hopeful light by your own friendly, cooperative, and encouraging outlook. When we help others find well-being, then harmony exists for us as well. (1, 7)

Your relationships and friendships are steadfast as long as you rely on your natural patience and diplomacy. Don't lose sight of your ideals, but never try to "teach" by insisting that others accept what you think would be right for them. Trying to dominate people always creates unfortunate consequences. You will also lose power and prestige if you become too critical, impatient, or intolerant of others' idiosyncrasies and weaknesses. (7, 8)

There may be a negative aspect to your nature that manifests as fretfulness, uncertainty, fear, and emotionalism. The spiritual path will always bring a certain amount of undesired and unexpected obligations. You may have tasks that are real burdens, but through these you gather the strength, unselfishness, and wisdom needed for your life's work. Learn to accept the responsibilities life hands you, without resentment and with loving kindness. Meet them with sympathy, understanding, and helpfulness, in harmony and balance with everything around you. When you feel like rebelling, take a moment to realize that you accepted many of the burdens because of your compassionate nature. Be nurturing to your highly sensitive emotions and learn not to act on impulse; decisions, once made, cannot be re-made lightly. Open your heart to all of humanity, not only to those near and dear. Reach out to help, but also learn to be dispassionate, and know that sometimes it is wisest to let others arrange their own affairs. (2, 3, 9)

For your best happiness, you must have people around you who return the same love and caring that you give so freely to others. Your emotions control you more than you realize or wish to admit to, so when the insensitivity of others causes you unhappiness or frustration you can become unbelievably obstinate, exacting, fussy, and unreasonable. Mood swings can take you from the heights of ecstasy to the depths of despair. When this happens, put a rein on your emotions. Realize that you are truly a noble person and live up to the best within you. Then, regardless of personal problems, you can find the ultimate spir-

itual growth and fulfillment that great teachers and humanitari-
ans have discovered. (2, 6)

VOWEL TOTAL 66

All that has meaning for you is based on beauty, truth, justice,
and harmony. Domesticity, ease, music, and serenity lie at the
roots of your nature. Your thoughts are wholesome, kindly, and
focused on love, optimistic expectations, and benevolence—in
both the material and spiritual sense. Disharmony is anathema
for you, so you do everything in your power to maintain peace
and tranquility in all areas of your life, especially your home.
You apply your sense of justice to everything you encounter
and try to right inequities wherever you find them. A very good
listener, your strong humanitarian leanings make you a refuge
and shelter for those in need of solace, and you feel a deep
sense of responsibility for the welfare of others. (1, 5, 11)

Friends and relatives enjoy your company and your home,
filling your life with constant activity. Your home, large or small,
will probably always be full. You are most fulfilled when working around others, and you open your heart and your purse to
anyone who needs a friend or a champion. Children, animals,
and those who are helpless especially appeal to you, and you
are too kindhearted to turn your back on anyone. (1, 9)

Helping Yourself with Vowel Total 66

Your talent for making others comfortable will bring its own
reward—you should never find yourself alone or without love.
You spread hope and courage wherever you go and, with inspiration and imagination, lift the spirits of those who are depressed. In fact, those qualities are your finest traits and, used
intelligently, they can make the best possible world for you. (6)

A comfortable, aesthetic environment, security, and elegant
living are the treasures of your heart, but the demands of your
Birth Path Number and vocational inclinations may temper the
realization of these desires. Allow your imagination full rein,
and seek opportunities to do things on a grand scale rather than

being content with a limited range of activity. Make your dreams come true, but keep your feet on the ground and don't allow dreams to take the place of practical activity. (6)

A trustworthy and loyal friend, you are devoted to those you love, and because of your irrepressible need to help others you may substitute the joy of serving others for personal love. You have a passion for salvation, and you will sacrifice all you have and are to bring enlightenment to one soul. Your sense of equality and justice is keen and you will fight fiercely to see it implemented for others as well as yourself. Your stringent ideals of right and wrong become more firmly entrenched as you grow older. Being a professional counselor could bring you quiet ecstasy because you love to give advice, to have an input into other people's lives, and to heal emotional scars. (3, 6, 9)

You truly love and care for people, but your intense desire to uplift others may manifest in an overbearing love, so you may be accused of being argumentative, stubborn, or intruding upon the lives of others. (4, 9)

Don't overlook the desires of those you want to help. You can assist others better by helping them do the things *they* want to do, making their own decisions and creating their own destiny, for spiritual growth and the strengthening of principles come from working through a situation, rather than having someone else do it for us. (6)

You have everything you need to obtain all you desire in life: courage, determination, purpose, system, good scheduling ability, but you may have a tendency to scatter your talents. You are always busy, but you keep your promises and fulfill your tasks. When you see something that should be done, you pitch right in and work until the job is completed. (8, 11)

You never allow doubt, fear, despair, or depression to cloud the sunshine of your day. You do not brood over mistakes in judgment, even those concerning marriage, love, or business, but try again and again, meeting whatever comes with your wonderful sense of humor. To you, life is a game that must be taken lightly, because you cannot afford to let discouragement or failure get you down. At your happiest, beauty and laughter surround you and your cheerful, optimistic attitude is a good example that radiates out to all you meet. (1, 9)

By following your Soul's urge, you have the ability to live on a very high level and inspire others to reach their own pinnacles. You find great joy in helping others maintain high standards of love, purity, and justice, and you must never allow the complexities of life to dim the wonderful visions you behold. Success comes easier when you discover how to balance your intellect and emotions. (6, 8)

CONSONANT TOTAL 66

You have a deep-seated urge to really know what life is all about. Let your imagination and wit work for you. Develop your sense of humor and your talent to use words effectively. The highest demonstration of your energies in this lifetime can be achieved when you find your own particular field of self-expression and turn it into an avenue for the enlightenment and welfare of others. (9)

People feel easy around you, and you make friends wherever you go. You are shunned only by those who do not understand you. Because you are sociable and amusing to be around, some may not take the time to see the strengths and wisdom underlying your activities and believe that what appears on the surface is all there is to see. Your philosophy of living is to accept things as they come, not worrying about the good and the bad, always remaining cheerful and optimistic, never allowing life to get you down. (2)

Elegance, beauty, and quality are honey and nectar to your soul, and your home is gracious and tastefully decorated. As a parent or foster-parent, teacher, physician, or anyone who cares and provides for children (not necessarily your own), you present the necessary security and nurturing needed for those under your care.

Truth and justice are your most outstanding characteristics, and you can see the positive side of even negative situations. Never one to break your own rules, you are loyal and trustworthy, helpful and supportive to those you love.

These traits enhance your civic-minded and idealistic nature. Instinctively filled with courage, optimism, and faith in the fullness of life, you have an inner assurance that you will fulfill your destiny and achieve your life's purpose no matter how many obstacles present themselves. Having an essentially practical nature, your most satisfying projects must have useful and tangible results. Life brings you what you desire without great effort, so you usually have enough money and security to spend time and effort on needful projects.

Harmony, beauty, and comfort radiate from your delightful personality, spreading serenity and calm wherever you go. You are a natural peacemaker and a welcome guest at any affair because you have an understanding of human nature and an innate ability to raise another's self-esteem. With your flair for the unusual, fame could very well come your way, especially if you work in radio, television, film, or any communications media. (4, 11)

Because you have this talent to dissolve melancholy thoughts and moods, people look to you for relief from despondency and gloom. They need your vitality, your charm, your wit and humor to chase the clouds away. Learn not to chatter superficially or give away too much from the depths of your emotions, but maintain your naturally optimistic, cheerful manner, and you will always be the focus of admiration. Your greatest joy comes from this generous giving of yourself, for you have found the secret of secrets: Service brings happiness, love, and deep fulfillment. (2)

People truly admire you for your idealism, so don't allow your high standards to be compromised. They are what make you vitally important to this old world. Pursuing your birthright to teach others to see beauty and goodness where there are difficulties will, through use, develop your own talents of foresight, intuition, perception, and hidden psychic powers. (2, 3)

The Negative Side of Consonant Total 66

Your aims must be spiritual and highly altruistic. If selfishness spins the web you weave, then irresponsible actions are your loom and you become a busybody interfering in everyone's business but your own. To keep yourself in the limelight, your conversation becomes filled with gossip, exaggeration, and superficial chatter. Demanding undue attention from those around you is egotistical, creates irritation, and could be your undoing.

If you turn aside from your cosmic path of responsibility, the negative side may take the way of self-pity and you may mire yourself in passivity. You may feel the vicissitudes of life have pummeled you so much that nothing you do is worthy and allow your exceptional potential to go unused. Without positive effort on your part to strengthen your love and desire for service, you could become dependent upon others instead of being self-sufficient.

Realizing you've slipped to the negative side is half the battle, and life can become joyous again by acting courageously. Develop your tremendous talents and put them to constructive use. If you don't let fear overcome you; you will find the freedom to fulfill your destiny.

FULL NAME 66

Expressing and upholding the ideals of honorable living—the inspiring and uplifting standards of God and humanity—is your life's purpose. The quality of your life reflects integrity, equality, truth, and justice; by example you teach these traits to others. You are blessed with a glorious assignment, to reveal beauty to the unenlightened, romance to the unromantic, and life to the depressed. You don't work for fame or glory, and the Master Number 66 in your name may be the only evidence anyone outside your sphere will find of your mission here. It may be that only those you touch will ever know they are standing in the presence of Cosmic Consciousness. (2)

Words are your medium and you could be fluent in many languages. With your wonderful knack of conversing with all people regardless of race, sex, or religion, and putting them at their ease, you have a natural attraction to the performing arts. Your showmanship and amusingly articulate command of words make you the magnetic center of attraction in any gathering. Most people find your tremendous personal charm irresistible, and you accept your popularity graciously. (2, 5)

Although you can be meticulous and strict, you also have a loving nature and are soft-spoken and even-tempered, with the ability to bring calm to troubled situations. You have a healing effect on people. Your suggestions and insights come from a sense of detachment and fairness; your objective approach gives the situation a fresh point of view and the solution suddenly becomes clear. (3, 5)

You have an inborn talent for artistic harmony. Plants, gardens, homes, and people bloom at your touch. You can create beautiful and useful things with your knack for color and line. You love home, family, friends, and enjoy the cultured life of music, poetry, and art both as a connoisseur and as a creator. (2, 3, 5)

In spite of your pacifistic nature, you'll stand up immediately against unscrupulous and unjust practices. Always be ready to give a lift when trouble strikes another down, for every good that you do is like a deposit in a universal bank. Dividends can return from completely unexpected sources, rewarding you with love, prosperity, the comfort of a happy home life, and a multitude of friends and well-wishers. (2, 5)

Your attitude is composed and peaceful except when you fail to uphold the ideals you know are right. Then you can become guileful, egocentric, reproachful, and worrisome. In trying to change others, you direct unwanted attention to them and so undo all you have been trying to achieve. Remember your love must be given to all people, not just to one or two. Spread your light and work for the good of humanity as well as for those to whom you have a personal attachment. (2)

Opportunities for Full Name 66

You are very enterprising and dislike the limitations of subordinate job positions. You enjoy self-discipline and excel in positions of responsibility and trust where you can create harmony and adjustment. If you use these natural talents constructively, you will indeed go far, and with great flair and energy. Your affability, magnetism, imagination, literary and musical talents, love of people, eloquence, and sense of humor are your tools of the trade. Use them well and there will always be the helpmates and friends around you who are so necessary to your happiness. (1, 3, 9)

Soothing the suffering, helping the helpless, and comforting the unhappy bring you rewards of tremendous pleasure. Because of your innovative ideas in these areas and your ease with others, your most useful friendships will be with those who are also interested in humanitarian pursuits. So, for inspiration's sake, seek out people who have a strong positive and creative attitude towards life and the ability to make a recovery when things go awry. (6)

Finding time for yourself may be a difficult task; your talents are always in demand, and you can never turn down a request. While being busy makes you feel special and inspired, remember to renew your own resources frequently to avoid draining your energies to depletion. Laughter is good medicine. Mix sincerity with mirth and success will follow. (6, 11)

Your artistic talents can be used to adorn the lives of others as well as your own. Any commercial or industrial pursuit that combines comfort, beauty, harmony, and the expression of love and companionship could well use your energies. Occupations connected with homes, religious and educational activities, social and welfare work, and projects pertaining to children, artists, literary efforts, or the social life of your community maintain your interest and help you to be useful. (1, 6)

You will do well in anything requiring quick thinking or intuition. Selling is a happy vocational choice because of your effective, articulate presentations, but you would be happy in any profession where tact, diplomacy, and dependability bring best results. Nobody questions that you would make an outstanding parent or guardian! (1, 3)

Don't fail to serve when called upon. Even though you have good earning abilities, you cannot be happy unless you follow your destiny of service to others. Duty is the basic ingredient in your life, but it will never be drudgery if you welcome opportunities to extend love and sympathy to people who need or ask for help. Because you command respect, give good advice, and can bring clarity to confusion, others gravitate to you for counseling. Use these talents as guidelines when seeking employment. (6, 9)

You have a variety of occupations to choose from. Your intuitive perception of others makes you at ease with many types of people, and you can use more than one of your many talents at a time, moving from one type of project to another with composure and fluidity. However, because you are so versatile, you could become a jack-of-all-trades and master of none. For best results, select at least one of your talents and put all you have into developing it. Your life may be lived in segments, using one talent for a number of years, then moving into another area of expertise and developing another talent. (5)

POSSIBLE VOCATIONS FOR 66

Advertiser, airline pilot, animal handler or trainer, anthropologist, architectural designer, attorney, author, broker, cartoonist, chef, chemist, columnist, comedian, commercial artist, composer, correspondent, costume designer, counselor, dancer, dean, dentist, director of youth group, draftsman, editor, electrician, evangelist, environmentalist, fashion designer, foster parent, furniture dealer, gardener; film, stage, or television director; hairdresser, healer, horticulturist, humorist, illustrator, industrial designer, insurance agent, journalist, landscaper, lecturer, librarian, linguist, magician; manager or owner of apartments, children's home or hospital, convalescent hospital, hotel, or rest home; manager or owner of museum, delicatessen, grocery store, health food store, tea room, restaurant, or resort; mediator, medical researcher, merchant, minister, nursery school owner or worker, personnel director, pharmacist, photographer, playwright, portrait painter, professor, psychiatrist, psychic, public servant, publisher, radio or TV personality, rancher, real estate agent, receptionist, satirist, school principal, social director, sociologist, song writer, steward or stewardess, student advisor, surgeon, therapist, tour guide, translator, union official, veterinarian, waiter or waitress. (12)

10

77—DISCIPLE
OR VAGABOND?

"Why do cats wash themselves? Where do flies go in the winter? Why do you snore when you sleep?" Jereme's questions go on and on, unquenchable in search of knowledge. With my own Birth Path 7, I understand something of the force that drives his Consonant Total 77. I want to share with him one of Kipling's rhymes I learned when I was a child, which has served me well through the years:

> "I keep six honest serving men,
> They taught me all I knew.
> Their names are What and Why and When
> And How and Where and Who."

77s are disciples-at-large who roam the world seeking fulfillment and illumination. No experience is denied them. They may try anything life has to offer, but judgment will be swift and sure. They will be required to either judge themselves, or to be judged severely for mistakes in thought and action.

This is the number of mystical powers in action, and the Soul's demand is to achieve enlightenment and wise evaluation transmuted into cosmic love through personal application. In their soul search for right judgment, 77s will be called upon to make an analysis of each experience and to choose, with full knowledge and understanding, those which are uplifting and rewarding. This is the lifetime for spiritualizing the material, and materializing the spiritual.

Silence is an essential ingredient for the welfare of 77s. Meditation and times of aloneness are very necessary to their spiritual and physical well-being. It is only in the silence that contact can be made with the Soul within; that contact which creates mental and spiritual expansion and the unfolding of greater concepts.

The 5 influence of the 77 may take them to the ends of the earth. Using their mystical inner wisdom, they seek to understand all kinds of people and their conditions. They are happiest when their activities bring about changes for the better in the lives of the world's inhabitants, whether animal or human.

The premise of Master Number 77 is: 7 + 7 = 14 = 5. 5 is the traveler, globe-trotter, loves experience. 7 is the hermit, contemplative, introspective. The Key Words for 77 are: Self-Emancipation Through Inner Guidance.

BIRTH PATH 77

There is no Birth Path above 66 in this century.

VOWEL TOTAL 77

Your heart's desire is to grow in wisdom and understanding through inner guidance transmuted into outward service. You are spiritual, usually psychic, with very highly attuned intuition. You have great inner resources to meet any challenge and are clever, competent, and versatile. Vitality and enthusiasm carry you forward, and you will always remain youthful in heart and spirit. (3, 4)

Your approach to life is intellectual and scientific, as your inner self prompts you to search out causes and demand to know "the reason why." It is in your nature to observe, dissect, and draw conclusions, and you cherish every opportunity to learn. You can become an expert or a specialist in any field that interests you. (1, 9)

Your desire for greater spiritual understanding may be reflected in your love of art, music, science, languages, distant lands, and new people. Thriving on the challenge of the new, the exciting, you thrill at all experiences, examining, and cataloging all firsthand adventures. You love the extraordinary, the eerie, the unexpected, and you seek it out, meeting many unusual people and finding yourself part of strange happenings. (1, 11)

Your heritage is complete and total personal freedom. While you are not selfish or self-centered, you simply feel your life is your own to lead, and you allow no one to interfere with your expression of it. You follow your own standards of conduct, which are usually not the same as other people's, and this makes you naturally discriminating in your choice of companions, opportunities, and environment. You enjoy being with people, but you feel a distance from the rank and file. You can find compatible Souls to call friends among intelligent, progressive, scientific, creative, and resourceful people. There is much of the nonconformist in your makeup and you do your own thinking where religion, politics, or social life is concerned, especially as you grow older. (1, 3, 6)

An ardent reader, thoughtful and contemplative, you are a clever conversationalist who enlivens any group just by being there. Any activity where humor and witty rejoinders make you the center of the crowd draws you. Even though you do not seek it (and you shouldn't), you may find yourself frequently in the spotlight, sometimes when you least expect it. Your pleasant nature draws people to you, both in business and friendship. (11)

Helping Yourself with Vowel Total 77

You are sociable, but study and research is your basic way of life. You are a visionary, drawn to the inner spiritual path and your thinking is finely tuned, subtle, mystical, and usually on the spiritually serious side. You have a deep Soul desire to study unknown forces, the strange and mysterious aspects of nature, and are attracted to mysticism, magic, and philosophy, excited by the study of psychic phenomena in others' experiences or your own. The world will benefit when you augment your search for Truth by sharing what you learn through teaching, writing, or lecturing on these subjects. You would make an excellent writer or philosopher because you seek larger concepts and spiritual interpretations, traveling where the average mind is unlikely to go. (2, 3, 11)

Change is good therapy for you, and travel is a natural rejuvenator. When you begin to get fidgety, fault-finding, or irritable, put your ingenuity to work. Seek out opportunities to travel, even if only for short distances, and find out about human conditions firsthand. Learn a foreign language, buy something new, do something constructive or innovative that will make a difference in your work and surroundings. Don't criticize or snipe at others for imagined obstructions to your progress. Look first to your own restless discontent for causes. The Soul evolves through love and loving actions toward others— cherish your resourcefulness and use it to make those you love happier. (6)

For you, moderation is the name of the game. You must learn to walk a tightrope between the happy-go-lucky 5 and the serious, noble, and sincere 7 in your name. You may be ambitious, but avoid scattering your money and your energies in too many activities going in too many directions. Too much diversity may keep you from applying enough concentration to current projects, so that nothing gets accomplished, or you become too busy to take the time for yourself that is so necessary for your well-being. (6)

Be alive, alert, and active, but create a definite, constructive plan for your life. And regardless of what else is on the agenda, make time to be by yourself, to relax, meditate, read, and be more quietly mental than actively physical, especially if there are important problems to consider. Doing this daily will make you more clearheaded and less apt to make mistakes. Become familiar with your inner Soul guidance, and allow your innate understanding and wisdom to develop to its fullest. (6, 8)

Governed by a keen sense of the ideal, you want every detail completed on your current project before moving on to something else. You have a rigid sense of how things should be and strive for perfection and accuracy, stretching your imagination and exerting your energies towards sometimes almost unreachable goals. Although others may find it hard to understand your zeal and expectations, don't lose faith in Life's ability to match your desires with perfect manifestations. (6)

You are at home in almost any environment and desire to be a part of what is going on around you, so the best chance to fulfill your goals is through groups or public activity where you can be part of the action, but not necessarily part of the management. Let your charm, cleverness, and distinctive characteristics create for you a specialized and distinguished position in life. Then when your dreams are realized, don't forget to thank or reward those who helped play a part in your success. (6)

CONSONANT TOTAL 77

Highly sensitive, you require frequent contact with your inner Soul to make life more fulfilling and complete. It is essential that you alternate times of activity with times of stillness for the sake of your health. Regular trips to the country or time spent in the mountains or by the ocean provide the quiet, peaceful atmosphere you need to rejuvenate. You can also find meditation and rest within the stillness of your Soul in your own room. (9)

While privacy is vitally important to your well-being, mental stimulation is a necessary ingredient in your life, and you need intelligent people around you. Charming, intellectual, imaginative, and witty, your interest spans so many areas you can converse on almost any topic, and you have extraordinary insight when it comes to understanding others. Popular and self-confident, you have much to offer those with whom you associate. Although you may seem frivolous or superficial at times, you have depths few people have probed. (9, 11)

Both new and ancient metaphysical and occult truths are revealed to your clear-thinking mind, and add to your philosophical wisdom and practical knowledge. Relying on your ability and Soul Force should become second nature during this lifetime. You meet the unexpected with an open and optimistic nature, expecting positive outcomes to all situations. The mind has the ability to create, transform, or destroy, so you must carefully watch the method and direction of your beliefs and thought processes. If you recognize that knowledge is power, it should take you far, especially along technical and mathematical lines. (2, 6, 7)

Diplomacy, sincerity, and trustworthiness characterize you. You move with a natural dignity, and people instinctively respect you, regardless of station or occupation. Happiness is a natural attribute of your soul, and besides, you are usually too busy and active to be sad. Because of your ability to turn any task or project into a delightful adventure, you are rarely bored and few people find you boring. Though your actions are occasionally impulsive, you are usually honest and irreproachable in your motives. (2, 11)

The Negative Side of Consonant Total 77

If you have a negative side, it may come out in insensitivity, impatience, disrespect, self-centeredness, and intemperance. You do not lack reliability, even though you must be free to determine your own goals and destinations, but you do enjoy stirring things up just for the heck of it. However, you always remain benevolent and helpful.

Your part in life is that of the active magician, drawing from the wisdom of your Soul to find the answer to the problems of humanity. As you analyze situations, you are aided by a keen ability to observe body language and interactions. You could be a sorcerer, but you would be wise not to indulge in sorcery. Let your meditations and activities develop your inner Self rather than any wizardry, for within you are reservoirs of authority and magnetism that draw people to you. (2)

You cherish a healthy body because it gives you access to the pleasures of the world, but do remember that you must keep a sound mind if you want a sound body. Be especially careful of, even avoid, any activity that leads to addiction, such as gambling, drink, sex, narcotics, tobacco, or certain kinds of food. You could easily damage your body and waste your talents, your time, your energy, and your intellect. (4)

The dual nature of the 7 and 5 can make it hard for you to express your true feelings. You can rattle on and on, talking superficially and noisily, or you can become introspective, secretive, and distant. If tempted to talk without thinking, you can cause yourself embarrassment or entanglements by launching into subjects which you know little or nothing about, or you can be witty at the expense of someone less adept at words than you.

You may tend to be secretive and not talk about things that are deep in your heart, but don't overdo it. You need a close friend to help you talk it out, someone to act as a sounding board, to enlarge your ideas, or to sound the depths of your pain and provide an outlet to the surface. If you become too introspective you may create a communication barrier with family, friends, and other important people. Don't emphasize the mental over the emotional. Keep them in balance or you can become anxious, unsure, high-strung, chaotic, or disturbed. Learn to offset your introspective times with more active participation in the multitude of beautiful experiences life can present to you, but don't go to extremes in either direction. (3, 11)

You have a tremendous gift for the world, the ability to help others find inner contact with the Soul Force that answers all questions and performs all miracles. Listening to your Soul's guidance will bring forth your inner strength, security, and courage to face whatever comes. Be watchful over your own emotional nature. If you become too attached to material things, or allow what others think to matter too much, tranquility will desert you, disappointment will replace fulfillment, and you will find yourself distracted, fearful, and pessimistic.

Books, people and experiences help you acquire knowledge and provide mental stimulation. Spiritual interests underlie the primary activities in your life, regardless of the form your religion takes. To obtain happiness and lasting fulfillment, you must use the powers of the 77 with great integrity and utilize the results of your labors to benefit humankind rather than just yourself. (9)

FULL NAME 77

Independence and fruitfulness in thought and action are the hallmarks of your life. Charisma, nervous tension, inspirational ideas, restlessness, and curiosity characterize you. Creativity is a natural outlet for your great enthusiasm and nervous vitality. Keep faith with yourself and uphold the best that is in you, and you will never be left behind.

In this incarnation you must develop your analytical abilities, to search beneath the surface of appearances and understand the causes and results of experience. You garner more knowledge from actual experience than from another's advice or recounting. The ability to see all sides of things makes you a wise counselor, and others seek your opinion and advice. You may be inclined to be too mental, so balance mental activities with some form of physical rejuvenation, such as hiking, aerobics, dancing, or calisthenics. (2, 10)

Past lives have seen many trials, and in this life there will still be many obstacles to surmount in your search for Truth. Your resolution to develop and grow in spite of personal trials, conflict, and frustration will return the greatest rewards. Every difficulty is an opportunity to learn and create new situations out of old sorrows. Each condition carries within itself the means to overcome, and your purpose in life is to learn these secrets, to share them with others, and in the process to gain understanding, wisdom, and discrimination. (2, 3, 8)

Accomplishments come through insight, courageous undertakings, carefully directed ambition, and willingness to release the outmoded for newer approaches. Trying to hold on to some thing or situation that should be put behind you causes stagnation, and you'll soon realize that life flows more smoothly when you let go of the past. (2)

As time progresses, you evolve into an unselfish, tolerant, and sensitive person with deep empathy and kindness and a sense of justice. Your greatest asset lies in your ability to deal with the unexpected, because you are not fearful and often are not even aware of potential dangers. You meet the unanticipated with poise and interest, accept changes with equanimity, and use them as opportunities for greater growth and wider experiences. Others may consider you out-of-the-ordinary, or hard to understand, since you are essentially a loner and follow unconventional lines of thought and action. Partnerships, even marriage, may present difficult challenges for you. (4)

Opportunities for Full Name 77

Your occupation must have variety and use your initiative and keen judgment of human nature. You get along especially well with the opposite sex. You are attracted to things of perfection, fine technique, and quality. You should find an interest in scientific art, and you could become a collector or an expert critic of art, antiques, or fields in literature. You are well adapted to any line of work that requires painstaking research and an investigative turn of mind. (6, 9, 10, 11)

Your career may change often during your lifetime. Vocations that express your creative imagination and fulfill your desire for the new attract you. To reach your dreams you will see many strange places and have many curious adventures. Life will challenge you, and your desire for knowledge will bring many unusual experiences and social exchanges that teach you how to distinguish between the real, the illusionary, and the superficial. (2, 6)

Fluent and expressive with words, you could become the most highly rewarded salesperson on the team, since your intuition tells you just how to approach the customer. You have fun traveling, especially to out-of-the-way places, and life would be dreary, indeed, if restricted to the confining routines of an office. It would be wiser if you were your own boss, for you resist taking orders and would rather go your own way, even if it turns out that your judgment was in error. You can always turn a mistake to your own advantage, anyway. (1, 6, 11)

You are a receptive, intuitive channel and mysticism is a strong force in your character. You may become a professional clairvoyant, medium, or psychic investigator. Your path will lead you into the scientific, the unusual, and the phenomenal, to discover and comprehend the mysteries of life. This will help you understand the hearts and minds of others. The best technique for your development lies within the silence of your inner mind; universal secrets are revealed to you through meditation, devotion, study, and prayer. Nothing is beyond your understanding when you learn how to enter into the inner substance of events and people. World religions and the study of Soul forces fascinate you. Research work in metaphysics or parapsychology may be more than a hobby. You have a natural flair for psychoanalyzing your friends, using some form of character classification. Helping people learn to live with greater use of their potential makes your life more fulfilled. (2, 6, 7, 10, 11)

Don't be unduly concerned with material possessions— your life will be comfortable and free from want. Whether this comes about through your own abilities or as the result of legacies or gifts, marriage, or some unusual way, you seem to be financially protected by strange turns of events, which allows you time for thoughtful reflection and opportunities to pursue your desires. Although this is not a material vibration, economic opportunities seem to arise in the timeliest fashion. (1, 7)

The desire for money usually does not play a large part in your choice of vocation. Planning, education, and consideration to put your special talents to careful use will serve you better than dashing into any field unprepared. Because of your need for freedom, your work should be professional, rather than business or manual labor, unless you have your own service or business organization. Use your intuition and psychic guidance when looking for the right job. (4)

POSSIBLE VOCATIONS FOR 77

Advertising agent, agriculturalist, appraiser, architect, artist, attorney, aviator, booking agent, botanist, broadcaster, chemist, civil servant, claims adjuster, composer, computer expert, counselor, critic, diagnostician, dietitian, drama critic, explorer, florist, geographer, geologist, government official, historian, hypnotist, insurance salesman or actuary, interior decorator, investment counselor, landscaper, librarian, magician, mathematician, merchant marine, metaphysician, minister, missionary, musician, navigator, painter, personnel director, philosopher, physician, physicist, poet, politician, psychiatrist, psychic, psychologist, public relations, real estate agent, satirist, scientific or technical researcher, singer, speculator, surveyor, travel agent, traveling salesperson, tour guide, translator, tutor, world religions expert; or anything in any line of communications such as cartoonist, correspondent, educator, English professor, illustrator, journalist, photographer, publicist, radio or television personality. (12)

11

88—CRUSADER OR FANATIC?

"I'm going to color this money green," Jereme asserted, as much to himself as to me.

"But it's a pile of gold coins," I protested, looking over his shoulder at a picture of King Midas staring morosely at his hoard of gold.

"I know, but green means it's growing and getting bigger," he replied and, bending over his coloring book, he was instantly oblivious to the outside world.

Well! This young man certainly has his own ideas about money. Not surprising, since his Full Name Total 88 should reflect considerable concern about the laws governing the making of money and how it should be used.

88s are an amalgamate of the highly motivated business executive and the intellectual, studious mystic. Out of this should come the visionary businessperson who does things on a grand scale, supplying humanity with the world's goods, while interested in high intellectual pursuits.

This Soul's demand is for self-mastery though Truth and responsible control of thought and emotions, which are the building blocks of the universe. Together they form the impetus for the experiences through which we learn the lessons our souls require. Our decisions made, right or wrong, teach us how to grow slowly and responsibly. 88s must consider the difference between emotionally motivated thought and thoughtfully motivated emotion.

The 7—88 reduced—supplies the thought power and the 8 supplies the emotional energy. Alone, the 7 is serious, studious, and inclined to solitude. By itself, the 8 spends its energy in the marketplaces of the world. Together, they provide a new arena of Soul growth, where thought and emotion must work together to determine how to change difficult situations and crises, to fulfill the vision of material and spiritual good for all the world's people, and to ensure high-minded aims for long-range enterprises. This testing, growing, and learning about the right use of material resources illuminates and disciplines both mind and body.

The premise for Master Number 88 is 8 + 8 = 16 = 7. 7 is the hermit, contemplative, introspective. 8 is the manager of money, time, resources, talents. The Key Words for 88s are: Self-Power through Self-Guidance.

VOWEL TOTAL 88

Your heart's desire is for power, prestige, and the best life has to offer. In your opinion, excellence is what really counts. You love things of refinement and quality such as classical music, rare books, beautifully constructed homes, quality clothing, antiques, and classic cars. Ambitious and enterprising, you have the enthusiasm and vision to go after what you want and to get it. You have an instinct for what can be successful; great accomplishments and accumulation of this world's good can be yours. (2, 3, 9)

Maintaining a high appreciation for honest business values is a must. Your tremendous powers of self-control, along with energy, courage, and determination will keep you going until you achieve your goal. You are efficiently organized, perfectionistic, and a keen judge of people. You have a philosophical attitude towards life, and at your best you are generous, altruistic, and philanthropic. You discipline emotional and physical urges and strive to maintain an "executive" appearance, priding yourself on your physical and mental stamina. (5, 6, 9)

Looked upon as a solid, respected member of the community, you are broad-minded, loyal, magnanimous, and sincere. You act responsibly toward those around you and are rewarded by their love and respect. (5, 9)

Along with natural dignity you have an air of authority. Taking charge of things comes easily to you, and you respond fairly and justly to any situation. You have sound, workable ideas, you inspire loyalty and respect, and you are a dedicated worker yourself. You have both ambition and personal magnetism, and with these you can inspire others to greater effort, pushing them to become successful by using their own abilities. (6, 9)

Your very highly attuned intuition, persistence, and intellectual and spiritual courage underlie your mental and scientific approach to life. An idealist, you are introspective and visionary, very attracted to the inner spiritual path. You'll find that teaching or writing on the subjects that interest you will not only increase your own knowledge but will aid in your desire to help humanity as well. If you live on the positive side of your nature, your life will be an interesting one and you will have much to give to others. (3, 11)

Helping Yourself with Vowel Total 88

Others may not appreciate you because, like an iceberg, the depths of your Soul lie beneath the surface. Although your life is active and busy, you must take time to get away from the jarring jangle of people and places to spend time in mental and physical solitude. It is absolutely essential to your well-being that you make time everyday to rest and relax—to think, study, and meditate—for here you shed the stresses of the material world and discover the depths of this inner Soul Self whose guidance will maintain you through all situations. Constantly seeking Divine Communion is a surefire way to consciousness-raising, and throughout this lifetime you'll often need to trust your Soul force implicitly. Do not lose sight of the benefits gained from following your inner inspiration, and you will always be in the right place at the right time. (6)

You have a keen sense of perfection and do not like to

leave a project until it is finished. You are not one to lose touch with your ideals, but sometimes you make life more difficult by trying to achieve too much too soon. Life for you must go at a slower pace. Your courage and persistence will pay off when you choose worthwhile purposes for which to work, rather than aiming for personal power. Making wealth the final aim in life will bring resistances and sharp disappointments. Much will be expected of you, so fill your heart and mind with the ideals that will carry you through. (6)

By background or karmic carryover, you may be hindered by personal biases which prevent you from completely fulfilling the destiny of your life. To overcome and eradicate bigotry, resentments, or jealousy you might look to become a healer of the body, mind, and emotions of others. You have a native talent for psychological analysis or research. To become a success in this field you need to develop an impersonal point of view and unconditional love for your fellow beings. Learn to understand and to be in command of your own emotions. (6, 8)

You are a powerhouse of energy, but you can help yourself immeasurably by realizing that little can be accomplished without others' help and support. Be lenient with the ineffectiveness and shortcomings of weaker and less competent people, and realize that this may be the best that they can do. Greater patience and mercy will make you a more positive and fruitful power for good. (3)

CONSONANT TOTAL 88

You are your own best friend, and solitude is no enemy. You know how to be at peace with your world, how to make the best use of your time, and how to be alone without being lonely. You feel akin to nature and you love the quiet of the country, with its orderliness, its natural aesthetics, and its seclusion and serenity, away from the din and bustle of the city. Quiet jaunts into the woods or a vacation by the seaside (if you can find a place away from the crowds) will give you the much needed time for yourself, by yourself. But you can also find contemplation and rest within the silence of your Soul because you know how to be still and draw strength from the inner recesses of your Being. (2, 3, 9)

Disharmony goes against your grain, and you give short shrift to quarrelsome people. You treat others fairly and demand the same consideration in return. Unshakable in your convictions, your attitude is one of faith based on positive action. You dream about accomplishing great things, things that also make life easier for others, and you try to fulfill the world's hunger for the better things of life. (2, 11)

Your ideal is to spiritualize the material. You will probably conduct any business or activity on a large scale. You think in global terms and could be found at the head of an international concern dealing with the betterment of humanity, where your novel ideas and good judgment can be used. You make a kind and considerate boss or overseer, but you are often disappointed when people do not live up to your expectations based on the abilities you see in them. Wealth and power come to you naturally and easily, but you don't put much philosophical emphasis on these, preferring instead the glory of a job well done. Whatever your work or avocation, you will be considered an expert in your field if you live by the positive influences of this Master Number. (9, 11)

You are surrounded by strong protective forces and possess an endless source of physical stamina. You are strongly courageous, but you should learn to exercise more caution. Courage is the ability to handle a poisonous reptile, but caution is the ability to recognize the danger involved and use a forked stick. (2)

The Negative Side of Consonant Total 88

Your feelings are deep and sincere but it may be difficult to find the words to express how you feel. Try to understand your inner nature. Knowing yourself gives you understanding and sensitivity enough to touch the depths of other people, and, with just a little effort, you'll discover you have a marvelous ability to help them bring out their own inner glory. (11)

You can be charitable, but you can also tell the difference between those who are truly seeking help and those merely looking for a handout. You may be short on patience with those who, although in need, apparently do nothing to help themselves. You have the resources to help them to help themselves, but you understand that doing it for them may be a hindrance. Your discernment will be enhanced when you realize that those with knowledge and ability can help themselves, but others less competent really need a hand up. Mixing the right amount of compassion with loving detachment allows you to work with deeply troubled souls while remaining on an even keel with your own emotions. (11)

You have a patrician bearing, a dignified and cultured manner, and possess a firm belief in your ability to face whatever the future brings. Look to the spiritual side for guidance or you may allow materialistic desires to cloud your good sense. Without compassion, unrestricted use of power could lead to misuse of that power. Revenge, indifference to others' needs, and conscious or unconscious cruelty could result.

You must use discipline and discrimination to curb the more destructive aspects of your nature, which awaken if your impatience or temper are not kept under control. You lead an active and industrious life and may tend to drive others as hard as you drive yourself. (2)

This is the lifetime to recognize the outworking between thought and achievement and use it in the physical world. The ultimate understandings that arise from use of Master Number 88 energies is that the material and spiritual worlds work together as one and that it is not wrong to use spiritual power for material success. Your lesson is to use success correctly, directing your accomplishments for the greater benefit of humanity. (9)

Using your energy competently and orderly is as necessary as effectively administering finances, if you want to get the most out of your capabilities. By putting the power of your thought to it, you can become a tremendous success, even achieve financial rewards, but the work you do must be directed toward the raising of consciousness and, consequently, the betterment of life on earth. (2)

FULL NAME 88

With this dynamic vibration you have a strong possibility of achieving authority, wealth, and renown. About you is an air of power, confidence, and strength that impresses others to expect you to lead. Here you have on-the-job training, as it were, for schooling both mind and body. Learn to live by the direction of your own Soul rather than expecting encouragement or sympathetic responses from others. Happiness, peace, love, and safety are human needs, but don't seek them outside yourself. You'll find them within, spiritual gifts that are free for the taking.

Self-study is the key to releasing the full force of your individual personality. Handling the mighty energies of Master Number 88 is a challenge to your evaluation skills—can you accurately assess your position in each situation as it arises? The best way to establish good judgment is to try to understand your motives. Philosophy, psychology, metaphysics, and the religions of the world also offer you keys to unlock the secrets of dynamically prosperous and fulfilled living. Your prime directive must be that which will promote human rights and justice. (2)

You do not accept anything until you can prove it or relate it to your own store of knowledge. When you feel you know the Truth, you have the ability to write, teach, or demonstrate that knowledge to others. You may investigate metaphysics, science, and other phases of the unknown as you try to understand the minds and emotions of men and women. By doing so, you learn to understand and to overlook the weaknesses found in human nature. Your life will be fun and challenging because your desire for knowledge will provide many adventures and strange associations to teach you the differences between real, lasting values and superficialities. (2, 4, 6)

If you don't live up to your best Self, your position and wealth can foster acquisitiveness and insensitivity to the plight of others. The undeveloped side of your character houses stormy powers of a savage nature that can destroy your peace of mind and that of others. Impractical dreaming and bouts with depression may plague you. Direct your energies towards positive living and let your intuition and imagination lift you to higher aspirations. Keep faith in your ability to think your way out of difficult situations. (2)

Reaching Master status does not mean there will be no more obstacles to overcome. The difficulties merely change in character as new truths arise to be recognized. Eventually you will become a gentle, loving, tolerant, and courageous person with compassion and charity for others. Real beauty of Soul with insight and a desire for harmony are part of your heritage, but you are still subject sometimes to the urges of your emotional nature, and you may find it difficult to avoid the lure of the senses. Take special care in your judgment of people so your romantic adventures don't have sorry or unlucky aftermaths.

You are active and creative with the possibility for highly developed mental powers. Practicing thinking in the abstract can create advanced philosophies which can be solidified through reasoning and writing. Devote your vitality to attaining your highest ideals, let your natural optimism prevail, and then serenity, comfort, and tremendous accomplishment can be yours. (2, 5)

Opportunities for Full Name 88

Your life may not be an easy one, but your triumphs will come when you apply spiritual knowledge to willpower and financial know-how. Don't dissipate your tremendous concentration and self-discipline struggling for wealth alone. When your projects are helpful to others, the financial end will take care of itself. Your accomplishments will live on in the lives and memory of others. When you work for the love of completing a task well done and find inner compensation just in the doing rather than in personal acclaim, the Laws of Karma are fulfilled. Then you can accept the honors that will naturally come to you graciously and without self-flattery. (6)

Deep within you is a heartfelt desire to improve the lot of humankind in every area of living: socially, materially, and philosophically. This can best be achieved by dealing with practical efforts on a large scale. Your natural executive talent and ability to manage resources could well find a home in industry, corporate affairs, or humanitarian groups. Such work will increase your effectiveness and the reach of your talents, along with your rewards and achievements. (2, 6)

There will always be a part of you involved with spiritual and philosophical thought that can bring about mastery of even the most difficult challenges. Opposing that is a side more interested in commercial, pragmatic, and material activities that work toward financial gain. Your most lasting successes come when you bring these two into balance, using wise judgment and humane responses with the physical world and its needs. Position and authority come from the proper blending of spiritual and physical forces. (6)

Determination and strength of purpose power your chariot of life. You do your best work in activities where thoroughness and specialized skill fulfill high standards. A career in mathematics, investigation, religious or scientific activities may use your talents. You could be successful in politics or in any activity that requires self-confidence, persistence, and the ability to make one's own decisions and keep the confidence of others. Your wide ranging talents can find success in any occupation requiring organization, computation, deduction, technical ability, or painstaking research, such as laboratory or statistical work. (5, 6, 10)

A good education is a must. You don't like to work with your hands, except perhaps in the making of delicate objects of art or technology or other artistic work such as painting, carving, etching, or glassblowing. Music or some artistic expression is in accord with your inner nature. In whatever you do, you should be a specialist, an expert, observing, analyzing, constantly adding more knowledge and deeper understanding of the work at hand, until people seek you out simply because you are the best and most knowledgeable at what you do. (6, 11)

POSSIBLE VOCATIONS FOR 88

Actor or actress, antique dealer, appraiser, architect, attorney, auditor, author, band or orchestra leader, bookkeeper, business analyst; administrator of hospital or other care institution; cashier, character analyst, church administrator, coach, composer, computer expert, contractor, corporation or tax lawyer, credit or loan officer, criminal investigator, critic, designer, detective, developer, dietitian, dramatist, educator, efficiency analyst, entrepreneur, estate manager, evangelist; florist, foreman, forester, fundraiser, geologist, government worker, historian, insurance agent, investment counselor, jeweler, landscaper, magician, mathematician, merchant, movie director, musician, nurse, office manager, philosopher, printer, probation officer, psychiatrist, psychic, public official, publisher, purchasing agent, radio or television personality, real estate agent or broker, researcher, retailer, salesperson, social worker, sports and athletic activities, statesman, statistician, superintendent, surgeon, technical expert, tutor, vocational counselor. (12)

12

99—ADEPT OR PIED PIPER?

99 presents such an exalted face to the world, one wonders if anyone will reach the 99th degree in this century. The holder of this Master Number must assume great burdens for humanity, guiding, demonstrating, and teaching charity, forgiveness, cosmic consciousness, and universal love. With irresistible charisma and a deep-seated ability to motivate others for good or ill, they are the teacher of teachers, the leader of leaders, and yet, if they would successfully fulfill their mission, their stance must be one of humility, serenity, and untouchable devotion to the higher good for all, sacrificing self on the altar of altruism.

99 must have spiritual strength equal to that of the great avatars of the past in order to endure the crucifixion of self that must take place within these noble, sensitive souls. They are empathic, compassionate, psychic, and emotional, and they approach the events of life with compelling power. The Soul's demand is for health and purity of mind and body, always working to free the individual from faulty practices and illusory beliefs, to truly know and act in Cosmic Consciousness. The followers of 99s are passionately loyal, but their foes would crucify them in a minute, given the opportunity.

Love is the Grand Master of the Universe, the fountain of life. If any human could love purely enough, if all negative reactions which restrict love could be banished, that individual would be the most powerful being in the world. Love will solve any problem, forgive any fault. No matter how great the mistake, the light of love is the most potent force for healing, the truest beauty of Soul.

Any missing number in the chart of a 99 will lessen the impact of total love, selflessness, and perfection. These persons may have taken on the potential of the 99 consciousness as a sort of trial run for future adeptship, testing themselves for Godhood. They consume the impurities of consciousness by enduring the trials of emotion created by self-centeredness and experiences exhumed from the lower emotions, and at the end of their life, they can arise like a phoenix from the fire of fleshly mortification, ready for the promise of immortality.

Since the 99s evolvement is nearly but not yet complete, their own limitations may restrict their range of activities. They might be preachers or missionaries in isolated areas or limited theologies, like the pied piper of old, drawing after themselves people who relate to their philosophy.

On the totally negative side, the 99s have as great a depth for evil as they have for good. They can delve deep into the study and practice of black magic, satanism, or devil worship. Fortunately, those who are currently seeking an adeptship in evil are distinctly in the minority, and it is to be hoped that in some lifetime, other values will supersede before the individual is is born to a 99 incarnation.

Nevertheless, we must remember that all creatures are made by God out of His own Substance. Therefore, even as they explore everything the universe has to offer, the inner core of light is never lost, no matter how deep it may be buried under centuries of misdirected energies. All experiences ultimately lead back to God, chastened, loved, and redeemed. This is the beauty of eternity.

The premise of Master Number 99 is: 9 + 9 = 18 = 9. 9 is the humanitarian, sage, counselor. Key Words for 99 are: Purification of Motive Through Selflessness.

VOWEL TOTAL 99

Your heart's desire is to raise all things and people to their highest form of spiritual, physical, and emotional perfection. Your wish is that every person realize and exult in the fulfillment that comes from doing useful and beneficial work. You freely give to all people the fruits of your knowledge, talents, revelations, and experience, without counting the cost. In fact, you would willingly give your life for humankind, if that would benefit the world. (1)

You have a great and compassionate heart, with a global outlook. Your destiny is selfless love and universal service, frequently associated with national and international movements. Idealistic, philanthropic, visionary, you are a great teacher and savior because your humanitarian and empathetic nature is always ready with kindly thoughts and deeds for those less fortunate than yourself. Patience, tolerance, and tact are strongly developed in your nature and you have no time to judge or control others. No matter how low the lowest caste, no matter how deep and dark the sin, you can always find forbearance, mercy, and forgiveness in your heart. (3, 7, 9)

You can also find opportunities to share your inspirations with others. You have an ease with words and people, a deep understanding of life, and you know that personal example is the best teacher. You strive for the universal consciousness and broadness of viewpoint that brings forth advanced ideals of art, science, literature, and philosophies. Your goal is to become adept in the practice of the divine and occult arts and through these to reach integration of mind and Soul. Long periods of silence and meditation are nourishing to your development. (2, 5, 9)

"You" is a more important word in your vocabulary than "me" or "I" because you think for others before yourself. You are graced with the purest qualities of compassion, and genuineness. You have intuition, wisdom, and real faith that all things will be provided for you. As a result, you have irresistible power to influence people to change their lives for the better when you stay with your inner vision of love and beauty.

Strongly drawn by the unseen worlds, you ponder all

things in your heart and depend upon your inner guidance to reveal the Truth to you. Your telepathic abilities often reveal other people's thoughts, and your sensitive feelings can be easily hurt unless you learn to look into the Soul Self rather than stop at the boundary of personality. (9, 11)

Helping Yourself with Vowel Total 99

So strong is the power of your thought that an impulse to action naturally follows, although you might have a tendency to become mired in verbalism—the discussion of principles that keep you from following through with the impulse. You can overcome this by striving to act from the Soul perspective rather than through emotions or intellect, using emotional and mental energies for positive achievement rather than being motivated by them. Plan your actions and act with purpose and all people will recognize you as the Universal Friend you want to be. (3, 11)

Within the secret recesses of your heart bloom such visions of loveliness and beauty for all the world that you suffer deep anguish for the cruelties and degradations around you. You are often truly distressed when you cannot bring your ideals to fruition. You have reached the peak of earth's evolution and must turn and lend a helping hand to those still climbing out of the darkness. You are receptive, broadminded, and eager to "be about the Father's business," but you are keenly disappointed when you or someone you love does not live up to the perfection you believe in. Swallow your disappointments and maintain your steadfastness in spite of obstacles. Perfection is a slow process and no one on earth has reached its pinnacle yet. Your job is to help, counsel, and inspire others with your own broad vision and depth of thinking. (2, 6)

Your very nature is unselfish and altruistic, but guard your emotions so you aren't torn to pieces by the struggle between your Soul Self and the conquering of personality needed to bring your message to the world. Learn to watch your health. Beware of giving yourself to so many people and issues at the same time that you work to exhaustion, or find your energies spent on so many activities that few results are obtained. This not only delays your own progress but dilutes the universal work that is your heritage. (5, 6)

This lifetime belongs to others, and only a life of service and benevolence, truly sacrificing the ego for the love of humanity, can fully reward you. This is the point to which all incarnations lead. You are a Master Soul come to serve the world, having provided the foundation in past lives by defining the meaning of true service: to be altruistic and impersonal, asking nothing in return except the inner knowledge of work well done. (4, 9)

CONSONANT TOTAL 99

At your highest spiritual expression, you offer yourself and your talents freely to others, and you find a supreme satisfaction in being of service. Through many incarnations you have met and triumphed over a multitude of personal challenges and problems, from which you have gained insights into human nature that qualify you to be teacher, counselor, and friend. You have an empathy with the misery and heartache of others, and many seek you for comfort, advice, aid, and protection. (1, 3)

The emotional and mental aspects of your nature are well-balanced, a noble conscience guides your steps, and truth and equality are the motivating forces of your actions. You strive for perfection, aided by intuition and a deep understanding of life. You are intolerant only of that which obstructs justice. Sincerity, creativity, truthfulness, and dynamic energy characterize you. All that symbolizes life within you is devoted to expressing universal spirit and truth. (2)

You will not tolerate prejudice of any kind. You understand and seek to teach that love cannot be limited to one person or one group, but is a greater and deeper experience than these. No one is a stranger because you feel that all people are members of one big, diverse family. You do not find it in yourself to settle down anywhere, but you have a kinship with all life. Your activities encompass all things, but you cling to nothing. (1, 2, 9, 11)

Music is a strong force in your nature, and composing music or writing songs that uplift others may be part of your way of life. Expressing yourself creatively in your chosen media is therapeutic. Your depth of human understanding may be revealed in some form of creative or artistic achievement which could be internationally acclaimed. (5)

Highly introspective, the mysteries of life and death intrigue you, and you are subject to many psychic and occult experiences. You respond to atmosphere, color, environment, music, people, and voices. Because of this sensitivity you tend to swing between the highs and lows of happiness and sorrow, but as you become more in tune with your spiritual mission, this moodiness should disappear, and great serenity will replace it. (2)

In spite of your introspection you are active, full of life and vitality. Gardens, the feel of earth in your hands, sunshine, and fresh air are a calming influence when you become overwhelmed by all the activities that command your attention. Your interests are so broad and varied, you will always have many irons in the fire. Since people are so important to you, you'll probably be a city dweller. If you are, it would be wise to make time in your schedule to escape to the country or take a solitary trip. Allow time for the digestion of the stimuli that bombards your sensitive emotional nature; this will keep your high aspirations and noble ideals from falling into the trap of materialism. (11)

The Negative Side to Consonant Total 99

If you have a negative side to your character, it may be that you tend to be too extreme in everything you do—too sensitive, too idealistic, too tenderhearted, too immaterial, too temperamental, too impetuous. (3)

Gentleness and beauty of Soul epitomize you. Yet if you cannot reach your goal or attain the state of perfection you strive for, you can become unsure of yourself, fearful, anxious, emotional, vacillating, even intolerant of others because they are not living up to what you believe they are capable of. This is a weakness in your character that should be guarded against, for you have such a wonderful ability to reveal the beauty in the unattractive, the worth in the unworthy, to uplift humanity and to promote culture and spirituality. If you keep your aspirations high, your achievements will be beyond your imagination. (6)

You have a warm and generous nature, but you can appear distant and distracted when intent upon some heartfelt project. Because of your deep humility, you may seem sometimes to lack in forcefulness, but no one should underestimate your power of attraction. Others are greatly drawn to your pleasant ways, your charming and winning personality. (6)

You can be the radiant center of any gathering because you spread a love and happiness wherever you go that naturally dissipates the gloomy clouds that may surround others. You are welcome in any environment. If you feel rejected, you may be allowing the negative side to color your personality. Romantic, personable, and delightful, your manner is so appealing that if you do not have a remarkable number of friends and supporters, then you are not living up to the potentials inherent within you. (11)

Arrogance and self-interest are serious pitfalls that can destroy the confidence and respect of others. Above all, you must develop fair-mindedness and justice, tolerance for and empathy with other people, to understand their needs and motivations. In no other way can you exert the true universal influence in your power. (5)

FULL NAME 99

Your spiritual goal in life is to be directly guided by Cosmic Consciousness. Love, tolerance, empathy, magnanimity, and service are the secrets that bring you honor and success. Art, drama, music, romance, and perfection are your avenues of expression and your thinking is lucid and intelligent. With your inflow of Divine inspiration the most commonplace activity is charged with beauty, grace, and purpose. You can represent the ultimate in humanitarianism, and the warmth which fills your heart for humankind frees you from such personality traits as condemnation, scorn, envy, gossip, or pettiness. (2, 3, 6)

The Master Number 99 represents global or universal consciousness. You will inevitably find yourself mixing with universal Souls in cosmopolitan settings. Radio, television, and other mass media hold no fears for you and could be the vehicle through which you use your tremendous power to uplift the hearts and minds of people and to arouse them to love, beauty, and Divine compassion for one another. (6, 7)

You have a distaste for small-mindedness and orthodox attitudes. You express the highest form of compassion, and your very essence is noble, philanthropic, and refined. Your understanding of human potential, broadness of vision, and depth of insight rises above prejudice of gender, race, or religion. Forgiveness for everyone is the supreme goal and ultimate lesson of your life. All experiences, tests, even failures, are directed towards this end. (5, 6, 7)

In spite of your deep love for people, it is necessary to remain impersonal in relation to individuals if you are to do your cosmic job well. While it is possible for you to have family and loved ones around you, you must learn to remain free from emotional entanglement to avoid draining your energy. Use your great cosmic love to find solutions for troubled relationships, but be able to detach yourself when needed. Love and companionship above ordinary mortals' understanding will come to you only when you discover that the highest form of love serves all rather than just a few. Clinging too closely to personal love, objects, or power could cause them to pull away from you. When you perceive and express love as an unconditional Cosmic Principle, then that which you understand will be returned to you beyond anything you could ever imagine for yourself. (6, 7)

If you do not live up to your best self, you may feel this is a heavy burden to bear. And, indeed, if you disregard your mission, you may find yourself alone and melancholy, knowing the depression that comes from leaving things undone. You may have a tendency to become withdrawn, unconnected, too reserved, or solitary. (2, 3)

Opportunities for Full Name 99

Although this is not a money number, one of your many cosmic gifts is financial protection. In some manner you are always in the public eye, and many occupations fill the bill. Education and medicine fit your talents well, but the arts, charitable or humanitarian organizations, social service, public and civic work, non-fiction writing, spiritual leadership, and occult mastery are fields in which you could excel and succeed despite great difficulties. You may express yourself through written words, music, or the visual arts. You have much to say and will not be stopped from saying it! Your message is important for the elevation of humanity, and you reach, encourage, and sustain many people. (2, 3, 5, 7)

No matter what your earthly profession, you will bring to bear strong psychic abilities and mystical intuition to fulfill your obligations. Never materialistic, your spiritual beliefs are rarely grounded in traditional religious concepts. (11)

You will do well in any activity where you can express your talents without restrictions, combining your personality and universal overview with your special gifts. Your inner purity of Soul creates a catharsis in others that transforms misdirected energies and transmutes their tendencies towards inhumanity into nobler ideals and purposes.

An occupation that requires travel would be beneficial for you. But no matter where you are, or what you are doing, life should have many fulfilling and exciting things to do. At any rate, you should never be unsuccessful. You can reach the highest pinnacles of success and recognition, and life will encourage your abilities to express and fulfill visions unreachable by the average person.

With this vibration, you must always work to bring out your best traits and talents, avoiding drudgery—this stifles your creative abilities. You have the capacity to reach your goals in any field you choose to embrace. Life has showered you with so many potential talents and gifts that in order to develop them and avoid frittering them away, you must stand for all that is fine, true, and good. As you grow in grace and comprehension, you will find opportunities to broaden your horizons and encompass wider fields of service. Wherever you can give freely of your love and empathy, you will be successful. Restrictions of place or opportunity don't exist for you unless you create them by believing in limitations. You can reach such a high state of mental, artistic, and spiritual development that you can be a source of inspiration to the whole world. (5, 6)

Famous, influential, and wealthy people should be among your friends, but folks of every type will be there for you, giving you help and admiration when the dynamic energies of your Being are directed into positive endeavors. You are an instrument of Divinity, not the source, so don't become smug or vain about your popularity. Guard your well-earned ability to remain impersonal and inner-directed; laziness or too much attention to worldly activities could divert you from your Heaven-sent purpose and cause you to miss the delight of uplifting, inspiring, and restoring the lives and hearts of others. You have the power to reach your highest aspirations in this lifetime. Make it so! (5, 6)

POSSIBLE VOCATIONS FOR 99

Any occupation that beautifies, architect, astrologer, astronomer, attorney, author, chemist, civic leader, columnist on world affairs, consultant in all areas of communication, counselor, dancer, dealer in health foods, decorator, designer, dramatist, educator, entertainer, environmentalist, film director, foreign service, goodwill ambassador, human or animal rights activist, humorist, hypnotist, inventor, illustrator, medium, missionary, nurse, naturalist, parapsychologist, personnel director, philosopher, photographer, physician, poet, politician, playwright, professor, promoter, psychiatrist, publisher, ranger, religious leader, reporter, satirist, singer or songwriter, social or welfare worker, spiritualist, therapist. (12)

Mastery

Be now the Master of your Soul,
Tho' lightning flash and thunder roll!
Reclaim the deeds of darkness done;
Live the glorious victory won!
Now let forgiveness cleanse the slate
Of anger, prejudice, and hate.
As glory withers winter's blast,
Love is personified at last.

BIBLIOGRAPHY

Many, many thanks to these authors for their help in clarifying this ancient science.

1. Campbell, Florence: *Your Days Are Numbered*, Marina del Rey, CA, DeVorss & Co. 1958

2. Goodman, Morris: *Modern Numerology*, N. Hollywood, CA, Wilshire Book Co., 1976

3. Greenacre, David: *Numerology and You*, (out of print) New York, NY, Lancer Books, 1971 (out of business)

4. Hitchcock, Helyn: *Helping Yourself With Numerology*, West Nyack, NY, Parker Publishing, a division of Simon & Schuster, 1972

5. Johnson, Vera Scott and Wommack, Thomas: *The Secrets of Numbers*, New York, NY, Berkeley Publishing, 1973 (out of print)

6. Jordan, Dr. Juno: *Numerology: The Romance in Your Name*, Marina del Rey, Calif. DeVorss & Company, 1965/1988

7. Lopez, Vincent: *Numerology*, New York, NY, New American Library, 1969 (out of print)

8. Mykian, W: *Numerology Made Easy*, N. Hollywood, CA, Wilshire Book Co., 1979

9. Roquemore, Kathleen: *It's All In Your Numbers*, New York, NY, Harper and Row, 1975

10. Taylor, Ariel Yvon and Hyer, H. Warren: *Numerology, It's Facts and Secrets*, N. Hollywood, CA, Wilshire Book Company 1956

11. Valla, Mary: *The Power of Numbers*, Marina del Rey, CA, DeVorss & Co., 1971

12. To the list of occupations at the end of each chapter came contributions from:

    David Greenacre, *Numerology and You*; Helyn Hitchcock, *Helping Yourself With Numerology*; Vera Scott Johnson and Thomas Wommack, *The Secrets of Numbers*; W. Mykian, *Numerology Made Easy*; Kathleen Roquemore, *It's All In Your Numbers*; A. Y. Taylor and H. W. Hyer: *Numerology, It's Facts and Secrets*; and Mary Valla, *The Power of Numbers*.

ORDER FORM

10% DISCOUNT on orders of $20 or more —
20% DISCOUNT on orders of $50 or more —
30% DISCOUNT on orders of $250 or more —
On cost of books for fully prepaid orders

NAME

ADDRESS

CITY   STATE   ZIP

COUNTRY (outside USA)   POSTAL CODE

TITLE	QTY	PRICE	TOTAL
The Bowl of Saki	@	$ 5.95	
The Development of Spiritual Healing	@	$ 6.95	
Education from Before Birth . . .	@	$ 6.95	
Illumination (VHS)	@	$29.95	
Intrance	@	$ 9.95	
The Master Numbers	@	$ 7.95	
Music	@	$ 6.95	
Psychic Power & Soul Consciousness	@	$14.95	
On the Road to Baghdad	@	$19.95	
Spirit of Change	@	$ 9.95	

Shipping costs:
First book: $2.50
($3.00 for Canada)
Each additional book:
$.75 ($1.00 for
Canada)
For UPS rates and
bulk orders call us
at (510) 865-5282

TOTAL	
Less discount @_____%	
TOTAL COST OF BOOKS	(_____)
Calif. residents add sales tax	
Shipping & handling	
TOTAL ENCLOSED	
Please pay in U.S. funds only	

❏ Check   ❏ Money Order   ❏ Visa   ❏ M/C

Card # _____ Exp date _____

Signature _____

Complete and mail to:

Hunter House Inc., Publishers

PO Box 2914, Alameda CA 94501-0914
Phone (510) 865-5282 Fax (510) 865-4295

❏ Check here to receive our book catalog